Praise for the work of Eduardo Garrigues

"At its intermittent best the writing competes with Robert Louis Stevenson (that at least would have pleased Borges) and there can be no higher praise for the writer of an adventure story."
—*The New York Times Book Review* on *West of Babylon*

"Without hiding his affection for Gálvez, nor his desire to recover and praise him as an attractive and valiant character, Garrigues avoids writing an uncritical beatification by presenting both the positive and negative aspects of a conflicted personality. His reconstruction of Gálvez reveals psychological authenticity of this historical figure while also depicting Spain's foreign relations during the period of colonial crisis."
—*Letras* on *El que tenga valor que me siga*

"Garrigues reveals a flesh-and-bone Gálvez. Ambitious, irascible, proud but also audacious and mindful of the safety of the civilian population during battle; he is also passionate in love, as demonstrated in his relationship with the beautiful Creole Felicitas de St. Maxent."
—*Culturas La Vanguardia* on *El que tenga valor que me siga*

"A detailed, pleasurable and well written novel on the period and the central character: adventures, loyalties, penury, treachery and love."
—*El País* on *El que tenga valor que me siga*

"Reminiscent of the best of Hemingway."
—Miguel Delibes on *Lecciones de Tinieblas*

His novel, *Lecciones de Tinieblas,* was a finalist in the Novela Sésamo Prize, and he was awarded the prestigious Pío Baroja Prize for his story "Artículo sexto."

"I Alone"

Bernardo de Gálvez's American Revolution

EDUARDO GARRIGUES

Translated from Spanish by Nancy J. Membrez

ARTE
PÚBLICO
PRESS

"I Alone" Bernardo de Gálvez's American Revolution is made possible with generous support from the Fundación Consejo España-Estados Unidos. *Muchísimas gracias.*

Recovering the past, creating the future

Arte Público Press
University of Houston
4902 Gulf Fwy, Bldg 19, Rm 100
Houston, Texas 77204-2004

Cover design by Mora Des¡gns
Photo cover courtesy of Wikimedia Commons
Map on cover by J. Gibson—From Maps ETC at the University of South Florida

19 20 21   4 3 2 1

For my daughter Maria, who helped me edit the English version of this novel.

The Congress of the United States has recognized Bernardo de Gálvez' contribution to the War of Independence, awarding him "US Honorary Citizenship." We should also acknowledge the decisive role played by the Creole militia from Louisiana, the troops from Cuba, Mexico and other places in Latin America who fought with Gálvez in the same war.

Following the Spanish General this multicolored and motley army crossed the Mississippi swamps and braved the storms in the Gulf of Mexico to conquer the strategic British garrison of Pensacola, anticipating the final victory of the Continental Army in Yorktown.

Contents

Prelude

At dusk on Sunday, December 28, 1776, a dense fog rolled in from the shores of the River Seine enveloping Notre Dame Cathedral on the Île de la Cité, blurring the buildings' contours. The Cathedral bells had already rung for the Angelus prayers when a horse-drawn coach crossed the Pont Saint-Louis and ascended the cobblestone-paved street towards the elegant neighborhood of aristocratic mansions.

In the carriage rode three English-speaking gentlemen. The tallest and stoutest man among them, whose knees touched the opposite seat, was Arthur Lee. Sitting next to him was Silas Deane, a gentleman of medium build with sideburns. Opposite them sat a round-faced, chubby-cheeked and well-shaven older gentleman with a twinkle in his brown eyes, Benjamín Franklin, who had recently arrived in Paris and was the group's leader. Having declared independence from England, the United States Congress had commissioned the trio to negotiate the aid of European governments in their confrontation with the powerful British armed forces.

The American Revolution's leaders, especially Commander-in-Chief George Washington of the impressively titled Continental Army, knew that the Americans could not be victorious against the British without the support of other nations—even with the enthusiasm and bravery of their militias that had fought the British to a draw.

After the French authorities, especially the Foreign Minister, Count of Vergennes, had welcomed the congressional commission, they suggested the commission seek an audience with the 10th Count of Aranda, his Catholic Majesty's Spanish ambassador to France. In international politics, the two Bourbon monarchies of Louis XVI (France) and Charles III (Spain) maintained familial ties, so the Spanish ambassador did not want to slight the French Foreign Minister and therefore granted an audience to the congressional commission. But Aranda was not prepared to deal with this unprecedented situation and did not have time to ask Madrid for instructions; He, therefore, decided to receive them on a Sunday at an off hour to avoid having anyone notice the men entering the embassy, especially anyone who could report this to the English ambassador to France.

As the Spanish embassy staff had been instructed to do, when the commissioners' carriage pulled up to the entrance leading to the count's magnificent residence, the porter opened the gate but told the coachman to circle around to the back of the building for their clandestine meeting. At the back entrance, a servant carrying a candle was anticipating their arrival. The servant led the visitors down dark corridors in utter silence to the study where the ambassador awaited them.

The Americans had heard a lot about the Spanish ambassador, who came from a venerable, aristocratic Aragonese family and had held important government posts after a brilliant military career. However, their host's physical appearance rather disappointed them. Having amassed multiple titles, Don Pedro Abarca y Bolea was a Spanish grandee three times over, but neither the count's figure nor his countenance reflected that grandeur: one shoulder was lower than the other, constant horseback riding had deformed his calves and his excessive use of snuff had disfigured the tip of his nose.

On the other hand, the ambassador, who perhaps expected to meet a bunch of shady, unwashed revolutionaries, found himself in the presence of three gentlemen wearing brand-new, dark waistcoats in the English style. This made him think the American Revolution had yet to abandon the mother country's fashions. The first to greet him—and the man who made the best impression—was the famous writer and inventor Benjamín Franklin, who was dressed simply and did not even wear a wig. Wanting to avoid any fussiness in his attire and communicate an easiness in his manner, Franklin had in fact thrown his wig into the ocean as their ship had approached the French coast. Although his facial features were rather plain, Franklin's expression was direct and affable, his eyes twinkling with wisdom and good humor.

The host and his three guests quickly realized they were going to have problems understanding each other because, as the ambassador later wrote in his dispatch to Madrid, "Franklin spoke very little French; Deane even less, and Lee not at all." Aranda himself only knew a few words in English. After introducing the delegation in broken French so that the Spanish ambassador would understand the motive for their visit, Benjamin Franklin took a rumpled piece of paper from his waistcoat pocket to recall the details of the proposed reciprocal trade agreement between the former English colonies and the French court. This was the treaty the commissioners had already favorably presented to French Foreign Minister Vergennes. Franklin added in halting French that they intended to offer it to the Spanish Crown as well. Although the Count of Aranda prided himself on his enlightened attitude, he almost fainted. These were representatives of a country that had yet to be recognized internationally, yet they were offering him the possibility of a treaty as if they were on an equal footing with His Catholic Majesty, King Charles III.

A seasoned diplomat, the Spanish ambassador tried to conceal his shock, which bordered on indignation. He replied to Franklin in his excellent French sprinkled with a few English words that he thought it was precipitous for the American congress to attempt to sign a reciprocal treaty, when firstly, the country had not yet become independent and, secondly, could not assure control over its own territory. He added his belief that, for the moment, it would be more logical to ask for European aid in exchange for some advantageous arrangement, at least until the conflict had been resolved. Given the radical differences in the men's mentalities and expectations, the meeting could have deteriorated into speaking at cross purposes, but both parties decided to chalk up the initial lack of understanding to language issues. They agreed they should postpone the next meeting for a few days until they could have an interpreter present. At that juncture, the ambassador courteously wished them good night and asked his assistant to accompany his visitors to the back door.

Aware of King Charles III's character, Aranda knew that the Spanish monarch would never officially recognize representatives of a country that had rebelled against their legitimate sovereign. He additionally surmised that Secretary of State Grimaldi would probably react in the same way to the Americans' aspirations. But since the count was paying several spies to inform him of happenings in Madrid and in other European capitals, he also knew there were supporters of the colonial rebels in Spain, even at the government level, if for no other reason than the fact that these American revolutionaries were eroding the power of England, Spain's traditional archenemy.

Aranda had already been informed that some cabinet ministers were using covert intermediaries to convey financial aid, arms and war supplies to the militias fighting against England. He also knew that in Madrid as well as in Paris not all wounds had healed from the humiliating defeat England had inflicted on them in the French and Indian War, which had taken place over a large expanse of North America. France lost all its possessions in the territory, and Spain lost the two Floridas and the island of Menorca in the Mediterranean.

Aranda knew that the cowardly Italian Marquis of Grimaldi, Spain's minister of state, would be against supporting the American commissioners. But with characteristic vehemence, Aranda communicated his conviction to the Spanish Court: Spain should recognize the colonial representatives unreservedly and declare war on England immediately. He argued, "There will not be another opportunity to vanquish England like this one for centuries."

"I Alone"

Bernardo de Gálvez's
American Revolution

Part One

CHAPTER I
The Road to Almadén
(Bernardo de Gálvez speaks)

After a long ride on that dusty trail filled with potholes we called a highway, south from Madrid to Andalusia, we arrived at Puerto Lápice. Accompanying me were Sergeant Melecio Rodríguez, a local shepherd who was our guide and a military escort of four halberdier guards. We turned off onto a narrower road, which, according to our guide, was a short cut to Almadén.

I was familiar with the principal route, having ridden once to Cádiz and back in the past. So I thought it better to travel to Ciudad Real using the same road southward as the carts carrying quicksilver in containers from Almadén. The ore would later be loaded onto ships bound for the Spanish colonies. It seemed as if Sergeant Rodríguez, charged by my Uncle José de Gálvez with protecting me, was deliberately bypassing towns where our armed halberdier escort might arouse local curiosity. Instead of the usual, well-traveled route other wayfarers frequented, he always chose the solitary, winding trails preferred by highwaymen and smugglers.

Since we had left Madrid, Melecio never took his eyes off me—or rather, he never took his one eye off me because the sergeant had lost his other eye to an arquebus bullet. This made me think my uncle had ordered him to keep me in his custody rather than to act as my personal security. But since I was still convalescing from the wounds I had sustained in the siege of Algiers, I would not have been able to give the halberdier guards the slip. The only thing that was certain was this unpleasant mission to the Almadén mines Don José had given me.

3

After I was released from San Carlos Hospital, I hardly had time to occupy my post in the new military academy in Ávila, when my Uncle José called me back to Madrid urgently.

There was no question of making my uncle wait. Apart from the respect I owed him as my father's brother, His Majesty the King had just appointed him Secretary of the Council of the Indies, so I arranged for a seat on the first stagecoach leaving for the capital.

Convinced that I had been promoted to lieutenant colonel after the battle of Algiers thanks to Uncle José's influence, I wanted to show up at his office dressed in my new uniform. I didn't have enough to pay a military tailor, so I hired a seamstress on Hileras Street to mend a uniform belonging to a colonel who had died—in the siege of Algiers, actually. I was grateful the seamstress skillfully patched the grapeshot holes in the dead man's waistcoat.

Don José did not make me wait long in the antechamber of his Buen Retiro Palace office and, true to his character that I knew well, he came directly to the point.

"Doubtless you'll recall that during my time as an inspector general in the New Spain viceroyalty, thanks to the intense Sonoran campaign and the harshness of that climate, I fell ill with ague."

Don José didn't wait for me to answer before continuing. "Do you remember too that my sickness, besides from attacking my body, wore down my spirit to the point of clouding my judgment?"

My uncle stared at me with his piercing black pupils and, as he continued, his voice shook with indignation. "I'm sure you'll remember as well that three memorialists were tasked with keeping a journal of the Sonoran expedition. Two of them behaved with the common sense and loyalty the circumstances demanded and with respect for the lofty mission His Majesty entrusted to me. The third, however, was disloyal and sent a memorandum to the viceroy about what I did and said while I was delirious from ague."

Don José was so angry, he could not even utter the memorialist's name without his lips burning: Juan Manuel de Viniegra. I am convinced that, with his elephant's memory, my uncle remembered that I had befriended the man, with whom I had long conversations while I was accompanying my sick uncle in Sonora. Once my uncle felt better, I was to join him and his entourage on the road to the viceroy-alty's capital, Mexico City. During the long journey, neither Viniegra nor I could imagine what trouble was brewing, once Uncle José found out the viceroy had received the memorandum in which Viniegra duly reported Don José's delirium. What my uncle had called "ague" was an attack of madness, plain and simple.

We had not yet reached Mexico City, when Viniegra and the two other memorialists were arrested and kept incommunicado, and all their papers and belongings were confiscated. My uncle ordered cat-egorically that none of those men who had traveled with him to Sonora—and had therefore witnessed his malady—were to mention it to anyone. When Uncle José tried to force Viniegra to retract the memorandum now in the viceroy's hands, Viniegra refused. My uncle had ordered him to be thrown into the ship's brig as a common criminal and deported to Spain; officials of the Inquisition had pre-viously seized copies of the Sonoran campaign memorandum. But, apparently before Viniegra was arrested, he had managed to hide the original copy. That was what was worrying my uncle.

"I have tried by all means possible to force the disloyal scoundrel to turn over the memorandum, but he is obstinate. When I was appointed the General Superintendent of Quicksilver, it occurred to me to send him to the Almadén mines, where we have him well-guarded, like all the prisoners who labor there. Even though for a time I forgot about it, it came to my attention that if after my appointment to as secretary the memorandum were to get out, it could do irreparable harm to my political career."

I did not need a divining rod to guess what my uncle was going to ask me to do next, although he hadn't mentioned it earlier. Don José knew perfectly well I had been friends with Viniegra before he was arrested, after which I'd had no news of him. What my uncle expect-ed was that I would go to Almadén and persuade the memorialist to hand over the document he had meticulously guarded up until then, despite having been threatened with torture and maybe even death.

"These pages contain the blueprints for opening the Almadén mine's new galleries. Please give them personally to the mine's superintendent. You know quicksilver is essential for the profitability of the gold and silver mines in Mexico and New Granada. Therefore, I recommend you visit the mine and learn how the ore is extracted." My uncle paused, his eyes once again boring into mine, before adding, "And since you'll be there, I don't think it's too much to ask for you to request the prison warden escort you to Viniegra's cell and, by whatever means you think necessary, persuade him to give you the journal he still has in his possession."

It was outrageous for my uncle to tell me to secure the memorandum "by whatever means you think necessary." It was obvious he had not recovered it by underhanded means, and now he was asking me to persuade Viniegra to hand it over to me by hook or by crook.

"I ask you to leave for Almadén as soon as possible because time is wasting," Uncle José added. "I've already ordered a man I trust to travel with you as well as a military escort to avoid any mishaps on the road to the port. I'm told the Ciudad Real wilderness is infested with highwaymen, who raid the carts, lured by the rich ore. But that should not concern you because the halberdier guards will accompany you. My only hope is for you to return with the memorandum in a few days. In any case, don't forget to visit me when you come back, because I've prepared a surprise for you that I think will be to your liking."

Past the village of Puerto Lápice, the trail we were traveling crossed an immense wasteland where the wind whipped up tumbleweeds. That distant landscape reminded me of those great desert expanses in the Viceroyalty of New Spain's internal provinces, including the uninhabited lands I had traversed at full gallop as I rode to see my sick uncle at the Cerro Prieto encampment in Sonora. As the sun flashed its final rays from behind the western hillcrest, the evening breeze spun the windmills on the hilltops in Ciudad Real.

I remembered that under similar circumstances the Ingenious Gentleman of La Mancha had mistaken those colossal stone and adobe windmills for giants. I mused that the ravings of that grotesque character who had tried to impose the laws of chivalry everywhere were not that different from my uncle's bout of madness. He had attempted to inflict his religion and customs on a handful of savage Indians using the same means of persuasion as Don Quixote had: the lance and the sword.

CHAPTER 2
Diplomatic Chess

Taking advantage of the Count De Lacy's brief stay in Paris at the Spanish Embassy, the Count of Aranda asked his colleague to attend the next meeting with the American commissioners as their interpreter. De Lacy, the Spanish ambassador to the Russian court in St. Petersburg, spoke English as well as French fluently.

The next audience between the Ambassador Aranda and the congressional commission again took place after hours and in secret, during which time the commissioners and Aranda had time to understand each other's position better. Aranda still had not received instructions from Madrid after his first meeting with the Americans. In any case, the interpreter's help was essential in pinpointing both parties' positions.

The Spanish Court was aware that Dr. Benjamin Franklin had been sent to Europe to solicit concrete assistance. However, Aranda insisted that Spain could not possibly sign a friendship treaty with the American Congress. Franklin replied that the situation in the rebel colonies was not so dire that they needed immediate aid. By signing such a treaty, the American Congress would see which European powers truly desired to be the new nation's allies.

On the other hand, Aranda verified that Franklin was not aware Spain had already aided the American revolutionary army by spending a million French pounds to purchase arms, ammunition and basic necessities and loading them onto the vessel Amphitrite. The ship had been chartered by a private merchant marine company commonly used as cover for the French and Spanish governments.

To convince Ambassador Aranda the Spanish court should recognize the colonial representatives and declare war on England, the American commissioners offered its army, as a trade-off, to help Spain recover the Florida territories ceded to England in the last war, including the towns of Mobile and Pensacola on the Gulf of Mexico. Thanks to his military expertise, the Count of Aranda judged this to be a very valuable proposition. He knew these strategic positions had allowed the British to do as they pleased not only in the Gulf but also in the Bahama Channel, thereby threatening Spain's supremacy in the Antilles.

When this second audience concluded, Aranda wrote another dispatch to Madrid in which he advised—on the strength of the deeply held conviction of a man who believed he was never wrong—that Spain should assure the friendship of the nascent nation by means of a formal treaty. Although the Americans had yet to declare a clear victory over England, this would give Spain the distinction of having gotten the Americans out of trouble.

The Count of Aranda next penned a letter to Secretary of State Grimaldi stating that if Grimaldi waited for the Americans to win before Spain acted, then he could not expect the new nation's gratitude for Spain's late and, in large part, secret support. "If we're to achieve any advantage," Aranda warned, "we must not employ insufficient, hidden means or secret aid, because these have little merit and will not appeal to the other party. . . . Time will be spent talking, and nothing important will have been achieved."

CHAPTER 3
Don José Casts a Long Shadow
(Bernardo de Gálvez speaks)

On the eve of our arrival in Almadén, we spent the night in a village called Hontanosas, north of the Alcudia Valley, at a dingy inn where our horses had to contend with the pigs in the stable to snatch a handful of feed. With a Manchegan accent so strong hardly anyone could understand him, the innkeeper bragged Queen Isabel of Castile had stayed at this very same inn during her pilgrimage to the Guadalupe Monastery. This made me think that either the royalty of the period had austere habits or that the inn had deteriorated substantially with the passage of time.

The innkeeper accompanied me to an attic with a low ceiling where, by the lantern's light, I could discern a rickety bed where he intended me to sleep. The bed seemed to have a life of its own, thanks to the multitude of insects and cockroaches swarming over the mattress.

I ceded the privilege of sleeping there to Sergeant Rodríguez, who was not at all disgusted by the mattress, perhaps because the army of lice crawling over his body could drive away a host of foreign parasites.

I preferred to lie down on the granite hearth in front of the fireplace, rolling up a blanket as a pillow and curling myself up so that the oak logs's crackling wouldn't singe the leather of my boots.

In addition to the hard bed not being conducive to slumber, the dancing flames in the fireplace reminded me of the bluish flames of our encampment's mesquite bonfire when I had been traveling with

9

Viniegra and my uncle's entourage on the road to Mexico City. The memorialist had waited until the other members of the inspector general's staff had collapsed from exhaustion to confide in me. That was how I found out what had happened in the middle of the campaign against the rebellious Indians in Cerro Prieto.

Viniegra thought that my uncle's frustration at not managing to drive the hostile Indians from their sanctuary, after having given them an ultimatum to surrender, as well as the suffocating desert heat, had depleted his boundless energy. Uncle José began to display symptoms of deep melacholy and ended up delirious and delusional.

After a night of insomnia, Uncle José believed St. Francis had appeared to him to advise him on how to conduct the war against the Indians. At dawn, he left his tent half-naked and summoned his aides, shouting about an infallible strategy to expel the Indians. St. Francis had advised him to "bring six hundred monkeys from Guatemala, dress them as ragtag soldiers and have them run through Cerro Prieto." This was the divine advice my uncle, the inspector general, had taken seriously at face value and was prepared to carry out unquestioningly.

As Viniegra told it, that same morning my uncle went to the barracks that housed a large number of troops and invited the officers and soldiers to take as much money from the expedition's war chest as they wanted. When one of his aides dared to challenge that decision aloud, my uncle threatened him, saying, "If anyone doubts my munificence, I'll land his head at his feet." No one dared contradict the orders of an inspector general appointed by His Majesty; an inspector general had even greater power over lives and haciendas than the viceroy of New Spain.

Uncle José had already demonstrated that power when, upon his arrival in Mexico, the viceroy had charged him with executing the royal order to banish the Jesuits from New Spain that had arrived months after they had been exiled from Spain. In some of the viceroyalty's cities, when popular protests broke out against this measure—which in many cases had deprived the disinherited of their spiritual guides, their teachers and their economic mentors—my uncle punished harshly whomever had participated in the riots. In all, the inspector general ordered the execution of eighty-five people, sentenced sixty-eight to a flogging and six hundred and four to life imprisonment. Around that time I had not arrived in Mexico yet; fortunately I was far from the place where those events occurred. When I again found myself with my uncle, he himself recounted in total detail the severity with which he had acted. He was proud of himself, believing that by executing the King's orders he was fulfilling the designs of Divine Providence.

Overnight, as I tossed and turned in my make-shift bed at the Hontanosas Inn, I pondered my relationship with Uncle José, the kind of rocky relationship that sometimes develops in tight-knit families. In principle, I should have been very grateful to my uncle, because thanks to him, I had left Macharaviaya, a hamlet in the Málaga wilderness, where my principal occupation had been herding the goats and swine that sustained our family of poor hidalgos. Don José had provided me an elementary education, had facilitated my induction into the army and, above all, had seen to it—through his contacts in the French embassy—that I attended the Cantabrian Military College. There, this open-minded and keen-to-learn country boy not only learned the French language, but also broadened his horizons. From that moment on, my military career was assured.

On the other hand, I thought that the long shadow my uncle cast had biased others against recognizing my merits. When I was promoted, as I had been after the siege of Algiers, everyone thought I had obtained the promotion thanks to my uncle's influence and not on my own. What made me feel somewhat more uneasy was that Don José had not thought to thank me when I had helped him get out of predicaments, such as when he had fallen ill during the Cerro Prieto campaign. When I was dispatched to keep him company, I had to ride out at breakneck speed across the enormous distance separating the Sonora province from my current location near El Paso del Río Grande where I'd been posted. As I had done whenever my uncle needed me, I did not hesitate even a moment to hasten to his side, traversing mountain ranges and plains infested with warring Indians, who easily could have ambushed a solitary rider. Once he had completely recovered, I waited in vain for a few words of gratitude or kindness in his recollection of my service to him. Perhaps gratitude was not part of his character.

When he indeed remembered me, on the other hand, it was to serve his interests in the sensitive mission to the imprisoned memorialist; he did not hesitate to send me to that remote location in Almadén, all the while knowing I was still convalescing from the wounds I had suffered during the siege of Algiers.

CHAPTER 4
The Ministerial Cabinet

In Madrid, Secretary of State Jerónimo Grimaldi received the encrypted dispatches in which Spanish Ambassador to France Aranda commented on his conversations with Franklin and his companions and gave his opinion on how Spain should respond to the congressional commission. The Secretary of State was about to be replaced by the Spanish Ambassador to the Vatican, the Count of Floridablanca.

Although Grimaldi had always maintained a tempestuous relationship with Aranda, and his point of view on this matter was radically opposed to the ambassador's, the problem was of such magnitude that he thought he should submit it for the consideration of the King himself before he resigned his post.

Once he had read the dispatches, the Monarch himself asked for copies to be distributed to members of the cabinet and summoned them to an extraordinary meeting so that all of the ministers could have a say in the matter. The council session took place in early morning and, before starting, Charles III announced he wanted to conclude the meeting before noon so he could engage in his favorite pastime: hunting in the Pardo forest. The cabinet members knew perfectly well the Monarch's opinion on the conflict and, although some of them were able to agree on certain aspects of Aranda's written evaluation, they tried to express their opinions in a way that would not contradict Charles III's point of view.

The information Grimaldi gave the council about the war between the mother country and its colonies surely came from the English ambassador in Madrid; it implicitly undercut Aranda's proposal: "We known the insurgents can't defend themselves and cannot resist the English army's onslaught. The British forces have retaken whole provinces and, what's worse, these negative outcomes have demoralized the Americans by sowing division and distrust among the rebellion's prime movers.

Grimaldi paused briefly to check if the Monarch and the rest of those gathered had understood his words, given that he was from Genoa and had a strong Italian accent. He then concluded, "Ultimately, I think it behooves Spain to entertain the colonies and help them surreptitiously, so as not to provoke England's reaction. We should provide them with what they need to continue to defend themselves without committing ourselves in any formal accord."

Next spoke the interior minister, Miguel de Múzquiz, who was a friend of Aranda's. "I agree with our illustrious secretary of state that the independence movement of the colonists is in its embryonic stage, and therefore they have roots too shallow to consider themselves an established country. I also agree we should help them because prolonging the war weakens our principal enemy . . . as long as England cannot accuse us of bias and deploy its superior forces to destroy our fleet and ruin our trade in the Americas."

In his attempt not to offend anyone, Muzquiz's words did not help the cabinet to come to a decision. The King shrugged his shoulders and next gave the floor to the Count of Ricla, the secretary of war: "In view of what Mr. Franklin has stated in his private audiences with the Count of Aranda in Paris, I am wholly in agreement with what my illustrious colleagues have expressed to His Majesty. It behooves us to do all we can to aid the colonists as long as we keep it out of the public eye. Only in the case of the English striking first should we declare a formal and public alliance with the colonies."

Next spoke Secretary of the Navy Marquis González de Castejón who, without openly supporting it, had the courage to favor at least a portion of Aranda's opinions in front of the Monarch: "We should not let slip by our chance to take advantage of the current difficulties facing the English. However, on the other hand, I should confess unhypocritcally that my opinion should not tip the balance in these affairs of state, for which I was not raised or prepared, although I'm convinced we should be the last kingdom in Europe to recognize a new, independent and sovereign country in America. Of that I have no doubt."

When José de Gálvez took to the floor, all the other ministers listened to him with special attention due to the conflict unfolding near Spain's American territories that fell under the secretary of the Indies' purview. Perhaps to ingratiate himself with the Monarch, Gálvez began by unleashing a barrage of invective against the Spanish ambassador in Paris: "Even when we can admit the rebel victory could, above all, wrest from our common enemy the domination of the seas in both hemispheres that they have usurped, I cannot approve of the Count of Aranda's proposal. Given his military past, he's always been more inclined to make war than peace, and, with all due respect, I think it's inconceivable for us to advocate for the two greatest European monarchs to sustain the creation of a new sovereign state in America."

However, thanks to his broad background in jurisprudence, Gálvez wanted to justify his opinion based on the law: "The first pertinent consideration would be to ask if the American Congress has a constitution, which obviously it needs. Therefore, for the moment, I do not believe we should treat its representatives as equals to us." Satisfied with having given the Monarch a solid argument to justify his distaste for recognizing rebellious vassals, he dared to sum up, "If I concur with our ambassador's recommendations, it benefits the French and Spanish monarchies to give the insurgents as much secret aid as we can provide, with the important aim of sustaining and prolonging the conflict until both parties annihilate each other."

The King took his watch out of his pocket so that the Ministers would notice he wanted to wind up the council meeting. But before leaving he informed the cabinet of his personal point of view: "Although we all know the rebellion of those colonies weakens our principal enemy's position, we should avoid adopting too complacent a position towards the insurgents that could allow rebellion to spark in other places in the Americas. However, that does not prevent our giving the congressional commission the support we judge necessary, as long as it is carried out in secret. And now, I pray Your Graces excuse me. I do not know if England's war with its colonies can wait, but the hunt won't."

CHAPTER 5

Valdeazogues (Quicksilver Valley)

(Bernardo de Gálvez speaks)

I had finally been able to fall asleep on the inn's granite hearth when Sergeant Melecio Rodríguez shook me awake before sunrise for us to continue our journey to Almadén. During the first two hours of the ride in the twilight, we had to trust our mounts' steady stride to follow trails so narrow they seemed more like paths left by wild animals in their mountain trek. At one point, I thought I heard a wolf howling in the distance, but perhaps it was a figment of my imagination sparked by my night of insomnia, or maybe it was only the echo of my own conscience.

When the sun finally dawned behind the steep hills, from the top of the ravine we could see the trail crossed a valley covered in vegetation. There, a stream of transparent waters wound past a thick grove of oaks, cork oaks and strawberry trees. Although the forest of Andalucía was somewhat different from the forests in the New Spain wilderness, the dense undergrowth and the strong current flowing down from the Almadén cliffs evoked the memory of my first expedition against the Apaches that the Chihuahua military command had entrusted to my leadership.

Despite knowing I had no experience in fighting the Indians, they had given to me—I don't know whether to give me a chance to shine or to see me fail once and for all—the difficult job of pursuing and punishing a band of Mescalero Apaches that were the scourge of the area, from the Ruidoso River wilderness to El Paso del Río del Norte. The heathens had recently attacked the caravans driving cattle and carrying merchandise twice a year to Chihuahua from Santa Fe, the provincial capital of New Mexico.

Beyond the village of El Paso, we entered a road bearing the grim name of "Jornada del Muerto" ("Route of the Dead Man"), it was so named because on that long stretch of the Camino Real there was nowhere the horses could graze and there were no springs where we could water them. We had to fill animal skins with water and carry them during the crossing so that the horses would not die of thirst.

Following the trail of objects that the Indians had stolen from the caravans and then thrown away, we managed to shorten the distance between us and the band of Apaches, thanks to the vestiges of their own depredations. From the branches of great cactuses hung bloodied women's dresses, empty powder horns and drums of firewater whose content they had consumed to the last drop.

Precisely when the riders as well as the foot soldiers had become confident we were nearing our objective, on the plain's horizon gathered enormous black clouds that unleashed a veritable deluge on the valley we were crossing. The downpour was accompanied by a storm of hail the size of dove's eggs, not to mention thunder and lightning that shook the earth beneath our feet. The squall was so intense that in just a few minutes the rain had soaked the soldiers' leather tunics and penetrated the canvas-covered vessels, ruining the pinole and toasted biscuits that provided sustenance to the troops. However, they were all so exhausted that, when I gave the order to halt and make camp, they lay down near the fire without protest, wrapping themselves in their damp blankets, too weak to chew even a piece of jerky.

Early that same morning, we found the Indians' campfire ashes still warm. When we resumed our march and were crossing a deep valley, we saw their trail on the other side of the river, a river that was swollen from the recent downpour. When we reached the edge of the torrent, after looking at the troop's emaciated faces that bore the downtrodden aspect of men who had not eaten in almost twenty-four hours, I told my aide to order a halt so that the soldiers could dry their rain-soaked tunics in the morning sun. The soldiers' murmurs of discontent reached my ears at the dry tree trunk where I had sat down to savor some strips of jerky. "We're hungry. We can't go on eating roots and vermin. Let's go back to Chihuahua for provisions."

On another occasion, the soldiers had returned to their barracks saying the Indian's arrows had killed their commanding officer, when in fact they themselves had cut his throat and thrown his body into a ravine for the buzzards to feed on. Therefore, I risked it all when I climbed on top of the dry tree trunk so my voice could be heard over the roaring stream and began this exhortation: "Gentlemen, the day has arrived to make the final effort to give the world proof of our perseverance. . . . The sky has unleashed its waters, causing us to lose our food supplies and soaking our ammunition, but if we go back in search for food, we'll be giving the Indians time to discover our tracks, and afterwards it will be impossible to catch up to them. . . . For us to return to Chihuahua having wasted time and money and having achieved nothing would be an embarassment for any honorable man. This ignominy does not fit my way of thinking. If no one wants to accompany me, I'll go by myself. I'll take a scalp to Chihuahua and make good on our expedition, or I'll pay the King's bread I've eaten with my life. Let the faint-hearted return and let those who want to share in my glorious deeds follow me in the knowledge that I can give you nothing except my thanks. Your good behavior will live forever in my memory and appreciation."

Without waiting to see the effect my speech had on the troops, I mounted and spurred my horse, forcing him to cross the stream. Soon afterward, I heard the other horses splashing and the foot soldiers crossing the current with the water to their waists, holding their guns above their heads so as not to wet the little gunpowder we had left. They followed me as one.

Without a moment's respite, that same night we fell upon the Apaches' encampment whose sentinels could not have imagined how a band of starving, tattered soldiers had been able to ford the river and climb the steep hill where they had camped. We killed more than fifteen Apaches, and a few more drowned attempting to cross the torrent; we took more than fifty captives, a herd of more than two hundred horses and a booty of finely cured buffalo hides valued at more than two thousand *pesos* at market.

I was totally absorbed in my memories of that adventure, when I noticed the valley we were crossing looked a lot like the one I had traversed with my troops while trailing the Apaches in New Mexico. The vegetation was somewhat different, but the grove had a thick forest of oak and chestnut trees, and there was a brook bordered by bulrushes whose heads were waving in the morning breeze. On arriving at the water's edge, the guide took my mount's bridle because the riverbed had thick, mossy rocks where the horses' hooves could slip.

When I dismounted and went to drink from the crystal-clear water, the local shepherd who was our guide knocked the tin cup from my hands before I could bring it to my lips.

"*¡Detener! ¡El azogue!*"the guide shouted. He warned me in his almost unintelligible Extremadura accent that the hazardous run-off from the mercury ore treated in the mines had contaminated the water. The sparkling creek, called the Valdeazogues, was poisonous.

Only then I noticed that the underwater pebbles were covered in a reddish patina that was surely residue from the cinnabar ore being worked at the mine. From the creek's surface wafted a foul odor, and among the rushes floated the bodies of several dead birds, including a beautiful royal heron.

CHAPTER 6
The Secretary for the Indies' Nephew

When the council meeting adjourned, Secretary of State Grimaldi accompanied His Majesty to the palace door. The others remained to gather up their papers and sip sugared water the butler had served. Since the last men to get up from the table were Secretary of War Ricla and Secretary of the Navy González de Castejón, José de Gálvez made the most of it by asking them to remain for a few minutes so that he could confer with them.

"Your Excellencies, now that the King is absent, perhaps we may speak among ourselves more freely. Without completely agreeing with the content of the ponderous dispatches from our ambassador to France, I do agree with him that the ambiguous policy advocated by this Court of helping the rebels surreptitiously while not daring to break with England would be dangerous. The inherent danger the ambassador points out is that with this policy we neither become friends with the Americans nor do we please the English, who surely by now are completely aware of our supposedly secret aid."

The two ministers exchanged knowing glances; it seemed as if, when the Monarch was out of the room, they were willing to express their opinions candidly. "If, as the Count of Aranda has informed us, not even the beneficiaries of our aid are aware we're helping them," said Ricla while attempting to conceal with his plump hand the smile playing about his lips, "they'll hardly thank us later."

"I think that the ambassador's warning is perfectly valid," corroborated the Secretary of the Navy. "Suppose the colonies win the war with England, then we'll find ourselves hand in hand with a new state whose rulers will hardly acknowledge that Spain had anything to do with their victory."

"Precisely because I'm no expert in foreign affairs," agreed Ricla, showing a warrior-like ardor that had barely emerged from his lips when Charles III was present, "I think excessive ambiguity doesn't usually yield the desired result. As Aranda warns, it could come to pass that we find ourselves with two enemies instead of one at the end of the conflict."

Neither minister could have imagined that their colleague, Secretary for the Indies Gálvez, like the bullfighter who taunts the animal before beginning the bullfight, was luring Ricla and Castejón into his arena.

"There's an important piece of information in Aranda's dispatch that not everyone has understood," clarified Gálvez. "The congressional commission's offer to help Spain regain dominion over the two Floridas and, what may be even more important, the control of Mississippi River navigation . . . That great river is the gateway to all the central and eastern territories in North America."

His colleagues did not understand Gálvez's intentions and they were unprepared to hear him speak so freely about a subject usually reserved for men trained in military and naval tactics. The two blue-blooded ministers exchanged dismayed glances upon hearing a *golilla*, an upstart minister—a civil servant risen to his high position by his own merits—lecturing them on a matter within their own purview.

Gálvez took advantage of their very surprise to conclude his argument. "Your Excellencies, I have become convinced that the Louisiana territory the French ceded to us in the Peace Treaty of 1763 is an essential strategic location for us because only in that territory do we have a border with the English lands to the east of the Mississippi River as well as with the territory north of the river that the American rebels occupy. Therefore, we should use Louisiana as a base of operations to deliver arms and supplies via the Mississippi to the northern states by channels so direct that the rebels cannot deny having received our aid."

Gálvez had succeeded in guiding his colleagues into his arena and, in bullfighting terms, he had waved the red cape at the beasts quite effectively. To complete the encounter, he only needed to lunge with his sword. At that juncture, the Secretaries of War and the Navy fell silent, hoping it would all soon be over.

"And if your Excellencies agree with this approach," concluded Gálvez, "you will also agree with me that we should name as governor of Louisiana a dynamic and daring individual capable of advancing the preparations for an inevitable war and, also, who can act as a discrete but efficient channel of communication with the rebel colonies."

Given that the man who still occupied the office of governor of Louisiana belonged to the Royal Navy, the Secretary of the Navy ventured to comment, "But it's my understanding that Luis de Unzaga, the present governor of New Orleans, is doing his job efficiently and has even successfully curried the favor of the French population, which was initially opposed to the transfer of the colony from France to Spain."

"That's true," answered José de Gálvez, symbolically raising the verbal sword before the kill, "but I've learned Mr. Luis de Unzaga is weary and has asked to be relieved of his post. I think we should take advantage of this circumstance to entrust this important mission to a young officer who has demonstrated his bravery and leadership on various occasions. Not only that, but also he'll get along wonderfully with the Louisiana Creoles because he speaks French fluently. This officer has just been promoted to lieutenant colonel for his heroic conduct during the siege of Algiers. His name is Bernardo de Gálvez."

Both ministers were indignant over the way their colleague had informed them, somewhat cryptically, of an appointment that fell within their purview, but neither dared to object, surmising that, by the way Don José had announced his nephew's promotion, he had already consulted the Monarch himself about it.

As Ricla and González de Castejón leaned over the table to collect their papers, they made a gesture like the one a humiliated bull makes when he bows his head so the bullfighter can sever the spinal cord neatly.

CHAPTER 7
The Almaden Mines
(Bernardo de Gálvez speaks)

Towards noon, when we pulled up in front of the walled compound of the mines, I had the impression it was more of a fortress than a mining operation. In reality, it fulfilled both functions, since from time immemorial the Crown had sentenced those convicted of serious crimes to hard labor in the mines. For that reason, the mine shafts' location was surrounded by an impressive stone wall, whose internal perimeter was dominated by a fortress that served both as barracks for the soldier guards and a jail for the miners. Because the quicksilver fumes were highly poisonous, working the mine was a slow death sentence.

When Sergeant Melecio Rodríguez gave the password to the guards at the heavy iron gate, Don Fermín Urrutia, the prison warden, came out to receive us. He grabbed my horse's bridle and held the stirrup to help me dismount. I was uncomfortable knowing that if I was being treated with so much deference, it was not out of respect for me or my military rank, but only because I was the nephew of Don José de Gálvez, the general superintendent of quicksilver, his highest superior.

As soon as we were alone in his office, I became aware Don Fermín knew of the nature of my mission because, when I handed over blueprints for the mine's expansion, he placed them in a drawer without looking at them.

"Thank you for bringing these blueprints to me personally. The mining engineers have been waiting for them to open new shafts. But

I do understand the real motive for your visit is to interview my accountant, Viniegra."

The warden surely noted the look of surprise on my face and said, "Although I keep Viniegra under lock and key, just as I do every other inmate, I thought it absurd not to take advantage of his knowledge. So I entrusted him with the supervision of the packing and storing of the quicksilver, and I must say, since Viniegra has been working as my accountant, not one ounce of the precious ore has gone missing. He's also housed in a somewhat more comfortable cell than the other inmates in the prison tower and, in consideration of his age and ill health, he also receives better rations than the rest of the inmates. Would you like me to have him brought here?"

"No, I prefer to see him myself at his workplace. That way I'll get to know the mine, something Secretary for the Indies Gálvez personally recommended to me. If you would be so kind as to accompany me, I'd be grateful if you'd give me an idea how the mining operation functions."

The warden bade me descend a steep stone staircase and through a tunnel leading to the mine's galleries, where a group of armed guards protected the massive gated entrance. From a distance, I could observe large, smoking furnaces and gigantic stills. But what impressed me the most was a reservoir of now purified quicksilver, the size of a large pool, brimming with the viscous and shiny liquid. Although the liquid seemed still, any occasional gust of subterranean air caused a ripple on the mercury's surface, giving me the sensation that at the bottom of that immense bowl a snake's rings were writhing.

"In that pond there's enough quicksilver to feed the mills of the silver mines in the whole of New Spain," said the warden, who led me afterwards to a subterranean passageway.

"To prevent prison breaks, we have dug this tunnel that goes from the underground prison dungeon to the mine shaft."

"So, the prisoners never see daylight?"

"The measure has become a necessary precaution. You can't even imagine the tricks and ingenious plots the condemned prisoners have come up with to escape the mines." His expression clouded over when, after a brief pause, he added, "... Although it's true that after spending years working in the mines, their fate is sealed."

Next, the warden explained to me that by breathing the poisonous vapors of cinnabar ore, the miners contracted an ailment affecting their motor skills, choking their respiratory tract and, in the final phase of the disease, triggering devastating convulsions like an epileptic fit. That's why those who contracted the disease shook like mercury ore, the *azogue* itself.

On the other hand, as the warden also explained to me, the ore extracted from that mine was an essential component for the mining of precious metal ores in Mexico and Peru. Therefore, the Crown followed with great interest the production and transportation of quicksilver, given that it indirectly maintained Spain's treasury. This relationship with mining in the Americas explained precisely why the Secretary for the Indies held the title of General Superintendent of Quicksilver.

Now in the mine's interior, the lack of sunlight, the contaminated air and the subhuman condition of the condemned prisoners, who pushed heavy carts through those twists and turns, brought to mind Dante's Inferno, except that my expert guide wasn't the refined poet Virgil but the gruff prison warden. The inmates who crossed our path seemed so absorbed in their labor and their physical exertion that they did not even notice our presence, as if we were invisible. Their faces were blackened by the ore, their limbs were eaten away by their exhaustion and, when they paused momentarily in their work, their whole bodies shook as if they were suffering a horrible fever; those were the typical convulsions of the *azogados*.

At the end of a long passageway, we arrived at a circular room where the memorialist who had become an accountant, Viniegra, was checking the contents of the bowls of quicksilver, using tin basins to fill up heavy leather sacks with ore. My proximity to the forge's anvil, where the accountant sealed the sacks full of ore with molten lead, reminded me of the gloomy atmosphere of that painting by the famous artist, Diego Velázquez, who depicted the forge of the Roman god, Vulcan.

CHAPTER 8
The *Azogado*
(Bernardo de Gálvez speaks)

Several years had passed since we had seen each other last in New Spain, but it wasn't hard to recognize Viniegra's hook-nosed profile, although his features betrayed premature ageing. The room's walls reverberated with the hammering of the miners and the screeching of the wood carts in the neighboring galleries, so it was impossible for the memorialist to discern the sound of our footsteps, but for some reason the accountant realized we were approaching and turned his head towards us. By the expression on his face, I thought that, despite the time that had passed since we had seen each other, Viniegra had recognized me. My presence in that place must have seemed so astonishing that a tin basin of quicksilver escaped his grasp and the slippery and viscose liquid spilled across the floor, causing a great commotion among his assistants, who hastened to retrieve the valuable product with the instruments at hand.

After rubbing his eyes, Viniegra got up from his stool and came to where I was standing and, unexpectedly, embraced me, exhaling his foul breath in my face and staining my chest with his drool and tears. When he finally regained his composure he dried his tears with the same dirty cloth he used to clean up quicksilver residue and told me, with the unsteady voice of someone who has lost the habit of speaking with his peers, "I know very well who you are and I can even guess the reason you've come to this inferno. But although I distrust the intentions of the man who sent you, I'm grateful someone from the outside world has bothered to come to this God-forsaken place to see me."

Viniegra gestured bizarrely with his hands when he spoke. I was shocked to realize those tremors were symptomatic of quicksilver poisoning. Viniegra was already an *azogado*. Although the memorialist could not ignore that my being in Almadén had something to do with the man who had persecuted and tortured him, I also guessed that my presence there reminded him of a happier time in his life.

I dared to say to him, "I hope you still remember the conversations we had during our long rides across the wilderness and the good times we shared chatting around the fire when we camped, under the stars and moonlight in the desert of New Spain."

"I've had no choice but to remember it because, since that trip, I've had a lot of time to think. Although the years do not go by in vain, I remember very well what your character and your convictions were back then. I trust you have preserved the sense of chivalry that inspired your actions."

Viniegra paused, as if trying to control his emotions and then he snapped at me firmly, "I can imagine what you've come for and, although it may shock you, I am prepared to hand it over to you without coercion. But before that, I'd like to speak with you alone without this pack of brutish hounds listening to our conversation."

Viniegra himself proposed we should be taken to the chapel located within the prison walls, where there wasn't the least danger of the prisoner escaping. The warden agreed. The prison chaplain permitted us to speak alone in the sacristy, a spacious room decorated with images of saints and apostles, although its walls exuded the same humidity as the rest of the building.

Once we were alone, I allowed Viniegra to vent all the bitterness churning in his bowels from having been unjustly persecuted for merely doing his duty, he insisted that his Sonoran expedition memorandum had necessarily included the ravings of the inspector general. The memorialist told me he had been persecuted simply for refusing to retract what he had written and, ultimately, for defending the truth. Although he could not overlook my kinship with his executioner, I could take the measure of the man by relating with humility and sincerity to the grievances and torture he had suffered, without attacking my uncle directly. I felt so small in the presence of that man's moral greatness that I never would have dared ask Viniegra to give me the original copy of the memorandum. But surprisingly, he himself was the one who gave it to me.

Without lowering his loud voice, that continued to reverberate within the sacristy's stone walls—perhaps to mislead anyone outside who might be listening to us—the memorialist approached one of the images behind the altar. It was a wooden sculpture of Saint John the Evangelist, which exhibited little artistic value but was very expressive, in it the saint was brandishing a volume of the gospel as if he were ready to slap any unbeliever with it. Climbing up behind the altar platform with unexpected agility, Viniegra removed a small penknife from his shirt pocket. With the blade's tip, he skillfully detached the cover of the book that the Apostle held in his hand; after a slight tug, the book's cover opened and a package wrapped in tarred cloth appeared from within the sculpture.

"Don't think I chose the book of Saint John's gospel for hiding my memorandum on a whim. In one of the scenes of the Apocalypse, one of the avenging angels will break the seal on a large receptacle, spilling its content, like quicksilver, on the ground. With help from the prison chaplain, I've been able to keep the document everyone's looking for right here. Nobody realized the most logical place to hide a book is to put it in another book."

With his fingers trembling, the *azogado* managed to undo the tarred wrapper and remove a thick manuscript bound in a sheepskin, whose vellum leaves appeared not to have suffered any deterioration in the sacristy. The memorialist ran his fingers blackened with mercury over the parchment's rough surface, as if he were bidding a last farewell to a loved one, and afterwards he offered it to me.

"Although this inferno's hardships may have impaired my judgment, I have enough sanity left to know that this manuscript is the cause of many, many problems for me. But it has also been my safe-conduct pass; your uncle's henchmen have not dared kill me without knowing where the document was hidden. Now, they would probably be doing me a great favor by ending my misery once and for all."

I was not proud of what I had done, but I was profoundly relieved to have completed a difficult mission without lying to, much less coercing anyone. My uncle had entrusted me to recover the document, and now I had it in my hands. After I managed a brief thank you to Viniegra, I left the chapel premises with the memorandum in its tarred wrapper under my arm. I ran into Sergeant Rodríguez, who probably guessed immediately that I had secured what I had come for because he urged me to take advantage of the moonlight and mount my horse, now at the ready. He suggested we depart immediately on our return trip.

If I had been able to speak with the warden, I would have asked him what was to be done with Viniegra, since the principal motive for his incarceration had disappeared, but we did not wait for him to leave the mine because the horses were already saddled, and I myself was anxious to get away from that inferno.

Hours later, when we camped in a forest clearing, I contemplated the campfire's dancing flames that reflected on the grove's branches above. I imagined monkeys dressed as dragoons climbing around the limbs of the oaks and the strawberry trees—as in my uncle's delirium—that could have served to drive out the Indian warriors of Cerro Prieto.

CHAPTER 9
The Ambassador Throws a Tantrum

"What can we expect from a Genoese Minister of State who doesn't even know how to pronounce 'horn' or 'onion' or 'garlic' correctly in Spanish?" sputtered the Count of Aranda at the peak of his anger to the Count De Lacy, who had helped him decipher Grimaldi's answer to the ambassador's dispatches, the ones in which he had informed him of the two audiences with Franklin and the other American delegates.

The Marquis of Grimaldi not only absolutely opposed as nonsense establishing an agreement with the congressional delegates but also the possibility of declaring war on England. He claimed all the cabinet members were against the war, when Aranda knew very well from his informants in Madrid that the cabinet ministers were divided on the matter.

As the ambassador was deciphering the content of the secret dispatch, with the help of his colleague based in Saint Petersburg, he was so overcome with indignation that he nearly foamed at the mouth. He tried to calm his nerves by sniffing snuff constantly and, when the precious little silver and porcelain box was empty, the count threw it to the floor to vent his rage. The box shattered into a thousand pieces. Afraid he would suffer an apoplectic fit, De Lacy asked the butler for a cup of chamomile tea with some drops of laudanum for the ambassador. When Aranda took a gulp of chamomile tea, he seemed to relax and in calmer terms commented to De Lacy, "The only thing that bunch of fools in the King's cabinet agree on is to continue sending arms and supplies to the rebel army on the sly. Regardless, it won't do us any good to spend our money on that aid, if the Americans themselves don't know about our efforts, as we saw the other day with Franklin, who didn't know Spain had collaborated in sending a shipment on the Amphitrite."

"As your Excellency well argued in one of the dispatches you were kind enough to read to me, if we don't support the colonists more openly, at the end of this conflict we shall find ourselves face to face with a rival in North America, instead of with a friend."

"Indeed, a new power bearing the noble name of 'America' with its two and half million inhabitants could, according to some sources, grow in no time to eight or ten million. The new republic will draw European settlers because the new state has attractive laws, and there are possibilities for expansion on a barely explored and undeveloped continent."

"What's worse, is that fool of a Genoese minister is telling me to limit myself to following the French court's lead in whatever Vergennes decides. Surely, you have heard me say that while England is our worst enemy, France is our worst friend. And from what I've seen, I am persuaded Minister Vergennes will follow the policy that will most benefit France without taking Spain's interests into consideration, which in this case are very different."

"Even for those of us not so perfectly informed about this question, it's now known the Saint Petersburg court has declared its neutrality in this conflict. For any perceptive observer, it's obvious the two Bourbon monarchies take different positions in most conflicts. After losing all its American colonies in the last war, France would have little to lose, while our possessions and our commerce with our colonies would be vulnerable to attack from the British fleet."

"I think the American delegates know very well that on this subject Spain's interests do not coincide with France's, but it's convenient for them to pretend they don't know that, and it's easier to put us in the same boat," Aranda said, sighing deeply after taking another sip from his cup of chamomile tea.

Suddenly, the ambassadors heard someone knocking on the office door, but, as the servant had instructions not to disturb them, he did not dare enter. He limited himself to wedging a small piece of paper through the door crack.

"Haven't I given orders that I'm not to be disturbed for any reason while I'm opening the dispatches from Madrid? I hope that note contains an urgent message because, if not, someone is going to get a caning."

The servant avoided the caning after Aranda read the note, which was signed by Mr. Arthur Lee, who asked Aranda to grant an immediate audience on an urgent issue.

"The gentleman who brought this note came to the door without prior notice and says he has instructions from his master not to leave until he receives an answer."

"All right, all right, you may tell the messenger I'll receive Mr. Lee at two p.m. today."

The Count of Aranda again asked the Spanish ambassador to Russia to accompany him during Lee's visit at the embassy. To that end, De Lacy's presence was providential, not only because of his skills as an interpreter, but because, in contrast to the other two speakers, he was a man of exquisite tact. While interpreting he knew how to mend fences between two people who were so egotistical and so unbending in their principles that they could end up in a shouting match.

According to what the Count of Aranda had found out, thanks to his network of informers that he maintained in several European capitals, Arthur Lee belonged to a prestigious Virginia family. His brother Richard Lee had presented a motion in Congress the year before concerning the separation of the colonies from England that, thanks to Jefferson's prose, would become the Declaration of Independence. Arthur Lee had studied medicine in England and had previously been named a secret agent in London by the same "Committee of Correspondence" that had appointed Franklin and Silas Deane as congressional representatives to the European courts.

Although Lee had been added late to the list to substitute for Jefferson, who had asked to be excused from the European trip due to his wife's illness, his dedication to the revolutionary cause as well as his reputation as a man of great intelligence and efficacy fully justified his appointment. His fine reputation in the professional realm, however, did not extend to him personally; everyone who met him criticized his irascible and belligerent character and his diabolical pride, which made it difficult for him to get along with his fellow congressional delegates.

When the servant led Arthur Lee to the ambassador's office, the visitor paused in the doorway for a moment. His great height and defiant look would have intimidated anyone who was not as brave a soldier as Ambassador Aranda.

"Please come in, Mr. Lee. My colleague, the Count De Lacy, and I have been waiting for you. If you don t mind, the ambassador will serve as interpreter of our conversation."

Lee curtly acknowledged the Count of Aranda's welcome. "Mr. Ambassador, I've come to inform you that my companions, Benjamin Franklin and Silas Deane, and I myself, believe it convenient for one of the three of us to travel to the Madrid court. Since we think Franklin's presence in Paris is necessary, I myself will soon have the honor of undertaking the journey. Therefore, I would beg you send a message to Spain announcing my visit as soon as possible."

Aranda thought for a few seconds and said, "Do all the delegates consider this step indispensable? Permit me to remind you that in attending to your delegation's petitions, I've already communicated your proposals to Madrid, although I am still awaiting an answer." (Aranda decided not to mention to his guest that he had already received a very negative response from Madrid concerning the revolutionaries' request.)

"Indeed," answered Lee, "we appreciate your good will and we know the Spanish court will follow very closely any position the French court adopts. However, although our conversations with the French minister and with you yourself may possibly be enough to satisfy the principal objective that brought us to Europe, we understand there are some particular issues concerning the relationship of my country with Spain that demand one of us be present in Madrid."

Although the interpreter tried to soften the commissioner's bluntness and tone, it seemed Lee was informing the ambassador of a decision that had already been made rather than requesting the ambassador's authorization.

Aranda noticed the arrogant tone of the speaker's words and shot back, "If you have already made up your minds, as I see you have, it's not up to me to approve or disapprove. Neither shall I attempt to dissuade you from your trip, although I think it would have been more judicious if you had first allowed me to propose it to the Madrid court."

Lee did not need De Lacy's translation to respond: "I've already received a free pass from Minister Vergennes to travel through France and, I would beg you, if you were to see fit, that your Excellency write me a letter of introduction as a safe-conduct pass for the Spanish authorities."

Although Aranda knew very well that Arthur Lee's visit would be a cold awakening for the Madrid court, it was no longer in his power to prevent it now that the French minister had given Lee traveling papers. In actuality, revealing the Spanish court's ambiguous attitude towards this American's inopportune visit to Spain had given the sly count personal satisfaction.

CHAPTER 10
A Well-Repaid Favor
(Bernardo de Gálvez speaks)

Upon my return from Almadén, the morning I went to visit Don José at his office in the palace, I noted something unusual: his pages were running in and out of rooms as if bearing urgent messages. I could not imagine the reason for such a hubbub, although I would be able to by the end of my meeting with my uncle.

"Here's Viniegra's memorandum on the Sonoran campaign, given to me in Almadén by the memorialist himself."

When I gave him the wrapper holding the Viniegra manuscript, with the same pride as a dog that deposits a valuable catch at the hunter's feet, it annoyed me that my uncle put it in a drawer without even opening it. So, I dared to comment, "Perhaps it would surprise you to know the memorialist handed it over willingly without my having to force him. It's not up to me to decide Viniegra's fate, but I believe that if he was wrong to hide the memorandum, in turning it over voluntarily it shows he should be reinstated. In my opinion, there's no justification for him to continue to be incarcerated in such a sinister place as the Almadén mines."

My uncle gave me a piercing look and in a high-pitched voice spat out, "You are right: it's not incumbent on you to decide that man's fate. But let me remind you that for several years he has besmirched your uncle's reputation and prestige, endangering a political career from which you yourself have certainly benefitted."

I could not refute that argument and opted to say nothing. When he saw I was no longer objecting, I noted that my uncle's expression changed, a smile playing on his face as he picked up a parchment covered in royal seals from his desk and held it out to me.

"It's not worth wasting time talking about the past when your future is bright: read this appointment letter."

The parchment contained a royal decree in which I was named colonel in the standing Louisiana Regiment. As Don José explained next, this was only the first step in having me named interim governor of Louisiana and later in my being promoted to governor of the territory. The news so completely overwhelmed me that I was nearly speechless in thanking my uncle for this favor. However, in some remote corner of my consciousness a little voice told me that by accepting the appointment, I would have to pay a very high price.

When my uncle saw how I appeared frozen, he rose from his chair and came over to embrace me. "Besides our family ties, I consider you the right person to take on the responsibility of provincial governor, although I must warn you that this position will not be a bed of roses. In the last war, we ceded the left bank of the Mississippi to the English and, although I'll give you much more elaborate instructions later, the goal is ultimately to recover the entire territory for the Spanish Crown."

"I thought we were at peace with England."

"Although up until now your predecessors in the governor's seat have maintained an uneasy peace with our undesirable English neighbors, I recommend you not dawdle but do what you must to control both sides of the Mississippi River by driving out the English."

"Before there's a declaration of war?"

"I would recommend you begin to harass the English before receiving official orders from the Court, because by the time war is declared, the enemy will already be on alert. I've chosen you precisely for this mission because I know you believe the best defense is offense. If you defeat the English, you'll have my approval and my reward."

"And if they defeat me?"

"Then you'll probably be court-martialed for acting irresponsibly and recklessly, and I shan't be able to help you."

Afterwards, Don José asked me to accompany him to the back of his office where, spread over a table was a large map of Louisiana, drawn by a French cartographer when that immense territory still belonged to France. The map illustrated the tributaries of the great Mississippi River from it sources in the north to the Gulf of Mexico. The map seemed very precise, drawn with the proverbial finesse of the French artists. The main river's banks and tributaries were marked with a fine green line, while the Great Plains and the barren land were colored in soft ochre tones. In the upper part of the map was the royal crest of the Bourbons and, in a side bar, an allegorical illustration of some slender palm trees and some equally slender, scantily-clad Indian women.

Don José allowed me to take in the map's beauty and let my imagination drink in the great waterway. Then, he demanded, "In a few months I want all that huge territory to be part of Spain's possessions."

With a pointer, Don José went about indicating places on the great river's left bank where the English military positions were located. "There are small garrisons at Baton Rouge, Manchac and Natchez to whet your appetite in your campaign against the English. At the moment, my information is they have not been fortified. The first thing I did after being named secretary was to establish a network of informers in the entire region. Our principal objective will be the storming of the fortified ports in the Gulf of Mexico, especially Mobile and Pensacola Bay. Now, we share navigation of the Mississippi with the English, but we want exclusive use of the waterway, given that we now own New Orleans, where all merchandise is unloaded."

Cupping his hands, my uncle added, "Imagine the Mississippi headwaters forming an immense upside-down bottle, whose cork is here below in New Orleans. And you're going to have the chance and the honor of uncorking that bottle."

CHAPTER 11
News from Paris
(Bernardo de Gálvez speaks)

At that moment, a liveried page entered the office after barely knocking, interrupting us.

"Forgive me, your Excellency, for interrupting this way, but Mr. Villepin, a secretary at the French embassy, is outside and says he needs to see you urgently. He also told me he would only take up a few minutes of your time."

Monsieur Villepin bowed deeply to my uncle and was satisfied with nodding in my direction, as he did not know me. I was aware the secretary of the French delegation knew Don José from the time my uncle had spent serving as an attorney for the French embassy.

"Monsieur Villepin, my page tells me you wanted to see me urgently. Would you care to tell me what matter requires such haste?"

The secretary began to stammer an explanation in Spanish with such a repulsive French accent that my uncle asked him to speak in French. Don José was completely fluent in French, and I understood French rather well after my stint at the French Academy in Cantabria.

"Your Excellency, said the secretary, you know I would never dare interrupt you, especially when you're previously engaged. Your friendship with Ambassador Ossun obliges me to speak with you in private to inform you of an urgent matter."

When the Frenchman referred to the matter's confidentiality, he looked at me and paused briefly, awaiting my uncle's reaction.

My uncle nodded to reassure him, "Villepin, Colonel Gálvez is my nephew, the son of my brother Matías, and you may speak in his presence with the same confidence as if we were alone."

"Pleased to meet you, *Monsieur le Colonel, enchanté de faire votre connaisance*," said the diplomat, whose obsequious manners were beginning to get on my nerves.

"A delicate situation has developed concerning the American commissioners that could affect French and Spanish relations indirectly," Villepin explained.

My uncle looked at the Frog impatiently, as if saying, "Quit beating around the bush and spit it out."

So the secretary put his hand into his waistcoat's inner pocket and took out a rumpled paper and held it out to Don José. "I thought your Excellency should have a copy of the letter that this very day Ambassador Ossun wrote to his Excellency the Secretary of State Grimaldi. The letter was written in reaction to a communiqué the embassy received from Paris this morning by special courier."

It took Don José just a few minutes to read the letter and to comment aloud, "From where I stand, a new, unexpected element has tipped the already delicate balance in our relationship with the representatives of the American congress. I see now that Arthur Lee, one of the commissioners, intends to come to Spain," said my uncle, returning the copy of the letter to the secretary. "I cannot keep a copy of correspondence that was not addressed to me personally, but as I understand, you yourself have given Ambassador Ossun's letter to the Marquis of Grimaldi in person. I'm indeed curious to know how the secretary of state reacted."

The Frenchman nodded expressively as if to underscore his required reticence on the content of that conversation, but afterwards he elaborated, "Your Excellency, I assure you I wouldn't dare repeat *mot pour mot* what came out of the Marquis of Grimaldi's mouth, *malgré sa bonne education*, in the presence of prestigious gentlemen such as you. Oh, *mon Dieu, quelle averse de jurons et d'insultes!* The least I can say is that the Secretary Grimaldi was extremely upset at the news of the American commissioner's imminent arrival in Spain."

"And do you know what steps will be taken to prevent the American commissioner from arriving in Madrid?"

Monsieur Villepin rolled his eyes and looked around, as if to reassure himself that nobody was listening, and then spewed, "From what I heard the Marquis of Grimaldi say in my presence, I deduce Monsieur Lee won't arrive in Madrid because he'll be arrested before he crosses the border or, if that's not possible, in one of the cities along the way, perhaps in Vitoria or Pamplona."

"So, what's to be done with him? Put him in a trunk and mail him back to France? Perhaps it has been forgotten: he's not a smuggler or a crook but a member of the American congress."

"I think that the good offices of a Basque merchant in Bilbao, one Gardoqui, who for some time has had dealings with the colonial rebels and who speaks fluent English, has been chosen to serve as mediator. Mr. Gardoqui will meet Mr. Lee en route and try to explain to him the reasons why his presence in Madrid is not convenient and, if it's possible, to convince him to return to Paris."

"At least Don Diego de Gardoqui was well chosen for this difficult mission. Now that I think about it, that's probably the reason I passed him in the palace hallway just this morning."

I understood then the hubbub of pages carrying letters and notes that I had observed while I was waiting in my uncle's antechamber.

CHAPTER 12
The Stagecoach Journey

Taking advantage of the merchant's presence in Madrid, it occurred to the Secretary for the Indies José de Gálvez that it would be a good idea to introduce his nephew to Diego Gardoqui so they could coordinate the delivery of aid to the American rebels from the port of New Orleans.

Gardoqui was preparing to leave on his mission northward to intercept Arthur Lee and give him the letter he had prepared in concert with Grimaldi, explaining why the Minister was not prepared to meet with him in Madrid. Simultaneously, Don José's nephew was also getting ready to leave for the northwestern port of El Ferrol. It occurred to Don José that if they each took the same stagecoach as far as Burgos, the merchant and the future governor of Louisiana could make good use of their time together to chat about how both their interests could be served regarding the colonial rebels.

From Burgos, Bernardo de Gálvez would head for the port of El Ferrol to board the ship that would transport him to New Orleans, while Gardoqui would travel the road to Vitoria or Pamplona, where he hoped to find the American commissioner on his way to Madrid.

As an Andalusian from Málaga, Bernardo had a happy and expressive disposition, while the Basque merchant from Bilbao, with his gaunt face and prominent nose, was much more reserved. Despite the differences in age and character, they got along well from the start and enjoyed each other's conversation, which made the long and dusty trip across the Castilian plain more bearable. They also took advantage of stopping at humble inns well stocked with blood sausage with rice and good wine from the banks of the Duero River. Along the way, they commented on the advantages and disadvantages of Spanish foreign policy concerning the conflict in North America.

In addition to being a smart businessman, Gardoqui was a seasoned diplomat. He confessed to the future governor of Louisiana that he did not agree with how the congressional delegates were being treated. "If the rebel colonists were to win the war," Gardoqui said to the young man from Málaga, "and the latest news we've heard is that the colonists have just won an important battle at Saratoga . . . When the day comes that they establish an independent state, the new rulers may easily forget what they owe the Spanish Crown. Lately I've had occasion to read copies of the letters the Count of Aranda has sent to the Madrid Court after receiving several American commissioners, among them Arthur Lee who's en route to Spain. Our Ambassador recommends that Spain recognize the congressional commissioners as soon as possible so that once the war is over, they will feel obliged to us."

Gálvez agreed with him on what Spain's policy should be regarding the conflict. Diego Gardoqui and Bernardo also directed their conversation to coordinating shipment of arms, medicine and supplies to the rebel troops, with the port of New Orleans to serve as headquarters. Although the sailing route would mean a long detour for delivering the materiel to New York or Philadelphia, what was certain was the British fleet was blockading maritime traffic along the east coast as well as controlling the Bahama Channel.

Gardoqui already had prepared shipments of several loads of clothing, arms and ammunition in Bilbao, and he arranged with Bernardo de Gálvez to have the frigate Atrevida at El Ferrol transport the new governor of New Orleans as well as barrels of gunpowder, crates of rifles and bolts of cloth for rebel uniforms.

Several days later when he got to El Ferrol, Gálvez found that the supplies and munitions that Gardoqui had promised him were waiting on the dock. He only had to sign the receipt and ask the ship's commander to load those bundles into the hold, indicating on the ship's manifest that they were part of the baggage belonging to the colonel of the standing Louisiana Regiment.

CHAPTER 13
Arthur Lee's Trip to Spain

While Gardoqui and Gálvez were traveling towards Burgos, Arthur Lee, having journeyed from Paris to Bayonne, crossed the Spanish border on Sunday, February 23, 1777 and hired a coachman to take him to Madrid for the very respectable sum of thirty *pistoles* (gold doubloons), provided the trip could be made in eleven days. It was obvious the delegate would waste no time in getting to the Spanish capital. Evidently, Lee had no way of verifying during the trip if his presence in Madrid was welcome or if steps had been taken to stop him.

The Marquis of Grimaldi, who did not know the delegate's travel dates nor his exact itinerary, expedited instructions to the regent of Pamplona as well as to the postmaster of Burgos to detain the American, but without causing him any trouble or inconvenience. They were to give him the letter Diego Gardoqui had prepared explaining to him the reasons why the Spanish government would be unhappy with his presence in Madrid.

In the diary he was keeping scrupulously during his trip, Arthur Lee commented on the difficulties of traveling on poor roads as well as lodging in even worse inns, among the other impressions he considered of interest. In Bordeaux, his agents had given him a letter written by his brother Richard Lee. Evidently, a Spanish general on his way to South America had informed his brother that the King of Spain was willing to give the United States proof of friendship; thus, the new nation could probably secure a loan from the Spanish Crown with better terms than anywhere else. This information no doubt raised the delegate's spirits, allowing him at times to ignore the harsh conditions of his journey.

On crossing the border, Lee wrote in his diary that "The passage of the Pyrenees is at first exceedingly bad, but when you get into Spain the road is good." He was also positive in his evaluation of Guipúzcoa's people, whom he described as "stout, well fed and clothed," and added perhaps to his surprise that "the women and men work equally the field."

In contrast, his observations on the Castilian landscape and peasantry were not at all positive: "Crossing the Ebro [River] at Miranda, you enter old Castile, where pride, poverty and dirtiness reign absolute. The Castilians have the complexion of Indians but are more ill-favored and their dirtiness and garlic render them more offensive than paint and boar's grease do the savages."

In his negative value judgment of the Castilians, the prejudices he acquired during his adolescence and youth in English colleges and universities were probably influencing him, because, although the Americans had rebelled against the mother country, they had not shaken off English stereotypes about Spanish inferiority and cruelty. As an American, by comparing the Spaniards to the Indians Lee meant he considered them the dregs of humanity.

A few days after Lee crossed the border, Grimaldi received a communication from the regent of Pamplona warning him that an Englishman named Arthur Lee had passed through Pamplona on his way to Madrid with a French passport and several letters of recommendation, including one addressed to the King's brother, Don Gabriel. Although this warning put the police on alert, they did not locate Lee until he appeared in Burgos, where neither Diego Gardoqui nor the outgoing Secretary of State Grimaldi, who wanted to meet with the American in person, had yet arrived.

Even when the postmaster of that city, in following his superior's instructions, turned over Diego Gardoqui's letter to Lee, a letter written with supreme tact and in perfect English, the suspicious and haughty delegate must have smelled a rat when he was detained. Fortunately, the Spaniard spoke not a word of English and could not understand the stream of invective spewing from Arthur Lee's mouth.

Gardoqui's letter, dated in Madrid a few days earlier, began by explaining to Lee that he had had business dealings with the colonies for more than thirty years, during which time he had always made the effort to be of service. Next, he referred to the delegate's mission in dealing with matters concerning the colonies and he tactfully warned him that in a city as small as Madrid, it would be impossible for him to remain anonymous. He spelled out verbatim that he would be spied upon "by an interested party" (alluding directly to the English ambassador), who surely would prevent the delegate from meeting with the ministers of state "without prejudicing the colonies' business in the extreme."

Gardoqui ended by stating that the outgoing Secretary of State Marquis of Grimaldi "was limited to His Majesty's views," but could meet him at a mutually agreeable place along the way and deal with any new business without the problems Lee's presence in Madrid might provoke. In the postscript, he specifically suggested they meet in Burgos and asked him kindly to wait there for him and Grimaldi.

CHAPTER 14
Conversations in Burgos and Victoria

In his laconic reply to Gardoqui's kind letter, Lee said he would wait for him in Burgos, without mentioning how upset he was at being detained on his journey as if he were a common highwayman. Prior to his arrest, he had even offered the coachman an additional six-doubloon tip if he got him to the Spanish capital two days sooner than they had agreed. At least, the American did not have to wait long, as Gardoqui reached Burgos the day after Lee's arrival.

Arthur Lee was beside himself at first, but soon Gardoqui's sophisticated manners and fluent English managed to calm him down. Lee understood immediately that Gardoqui would be his best ally in achieving his objective. So, while waiting for Secretary of State Grimaldi to arrive, Lee decided to make the best of an awkward situation.

When Grimaldi did arrive at the inn, they sat down at a candle-lit table and dealt with many issues. A tug-of-war ensued in which each of them defended practically irreconcilable positions. Lee wanted Spain to recognize the new nation's independence and declare publicly in its favor, indicating that recognition would be of much greater value to the colonies than the aid Spain and France were giving surreptitiously. He also gave Grimaldi a brief he had already prepared in which he argued that the neutrality of Spain and France left Great Britain a free hand to operate at full tilt.

Grimaldi defended himself, alleging that it was not the right time to declare war on England because France was not prepared to do so, and Spain was already committed to attacking Portugal. Despite their governments' official positions, Grimaldi insisted that offering Lee material and financial aid was, at that point, of equal or greater importance than political recognition. Finally, Lee was candid enough with Grimaldi to confess that the Continental Army was suffering serious shortages not only of arms and ammunition, but of commonly used goods such as blankets, needles, anchors, etc. He also knew the Spanish government had a guilty conscience for having refused to receive him. He further understood that, if he could control his temper, he would benefit from the situation, at least in material terms. Three thousand barrels of gunpowder and other supplies had already been delivered to the port of New Orleans for the rebels, but Arthur Lee requested another long list of urgently needed supplies from Gardoqui:

> anchors for 36-canon ships
> 24-inch caliber artillery
> artillery shells
> canvas for sails
> all kinds of rigging
> rope for tents
> muslin for shirts
> cloth for waistcoats and breeches
> blankets
> needles and thread
> white and yellow buttons
> shoes and stockings
> hats
> flintlocks
> sheet lead, copper, iron, and tin
> rifles, bayonets, and gunpowder

Grimaldi acceded to everything and, as compensation, Lee once again offered to have his army retake Pensacola and the Florida peninsula, and then cede them to Spain. He also promised that the dominions of Central and South America belonging to the Spanish Crown would not be touched. In closing, he assured Grimaldi that the United States Congress had authorized him to make these overtures.

After several days of exhausting debate that began at the inn in Burgos and continued for days afterward in Vitoria, the former Secretary of State Grimaldi and the American delegate Lee bade each other farewell without either of them having completely fulfilled his objectives. However, each had achieved relatively positive results to present to their superiors from their meetings. Grimaldi left for Rome with the satisfaction of having performed one last service for the Crown as secretary of state. Although Arthur Lee had not succeeded in convincing the Spanish government to side with the young nation openly and declare war on England, he returned to Paris with Spain's specific promises of financial aid and the shipment of supplies necessary to resist the English.

Upon his return to Paris, Arthur Lee would send a written summary of what was agreed upon to the new Spanish Secretary of State Count of Floridablanca. In it, he would stipulate that the Americans understood that, for the time being, Spain could not offer an alliance, but that Spain would aid the Americans with goods to be sent by Gardoqui's company to New Orleans, where the rebel army would pick them up.

Paradoxically, the one who had the most to lose from the start of the negotiations between the Spanish Crown and the American colonies was the Count of Aranda. Before leaving Madrid, Grimaldi had succeeded in convincing the King that not only did Aranda have knowledge of Arthur Lee's inopportune visit to Spain but that the trip had been Ambassador Aranda's own initiative, which angered the Monarch. The King then sent instructions to the new Secretary of State Floridablanca to exclude Aranda from any future discussion of the conflict in North America. Floridablanca shared his predecessor's animosity towards Aranda and had no qualms about sending Aranda clear instructions to desist: "As far as your back-door handling of the revolutionary delegates residing in Paris goes, His Majesty thinks it is appropriate for the honorable Count of Vergennes to deal with them exclusively and have the French Ambassador in Madrid inform our government on the matter."

PART TWO

CHAPTER 15
The Father of Waters
(Felícitas de St. Maxent speaks)

For several nights now, I've been waking feeling a profound malaise and have been tossing and turning in bed unable to fall asleep until dawn. The worst thing is I can't put my finger on why. Sometimes, when I wake up, I find that I am touching myself without realizing it. I don't think my insomnia is due to missing the pleasure that had been given to me by my deceased husband, Jean Baptiste Honoré d'Estréhan. When we were married, Jean Baptiste was already an older man, but his gentleness and experience in love more than made up for the vigor and passion a younger husband might have offered me.

Two years have already gone by since my husband's passing and, although a few distinguished gentlemen have courted me, up until now I have not felt lonely. Our daughter Adelaide is two years old. The idea of depending on a man again has even horrified me. In New Orleans society, the situation of a young widow with a rich father is enviable because I have a lot of freedom and few obligations. Perhaps the most discomfiting thing is having to shoo away the bees buzzing around me constantly at every festive occasion or while I stroll through the city. They do not anger me, because I knew how to clip their wings with a categorical, "No." The French language is very helpful in allowing me to be firm without having to use vulgarity. Probably other women in my situation would accept these dalliances just to pass the time, but I cannot let myself do that, above all because of the bad example any frivolous behavior may set for my younger sisters and even for my daughter.

When I began suffering bouts of insomnia, my principle of behaving honestly and prudently did not quiet the profound malaise I was feeling, an uneasiness more difficult to calm than any mere feminine desires. Although I was only twenty-two years old then and still had my whole life ahead of me, sometimes I asked myself what I was going to do with my life.

Should I remain in my father's house in New Orleans as a colorful, porcelain figurine like the ones adorning salon bookshelves, fading away day by day as the beautiful orchids fade in the garden? Should I leave the colony and make a new life in France, busying myself with the not inconsiderable inheritance my husband left to little Adelaide?

When the Louisiana Territory passed from French hands to Spain, some of our compatriots returned to our country, while others remained in the colony unwillingly, leading revolts against the new colonial administration and going so far as to banish the first Spanish governor, Antonio Ulloa, from New Orleans. But that rebellion did not last long and, when governor Alejandro O'Reilly arrived in New Orleans, he re-established order with a firm hand, with the help of some citizens of French origin, such as my own father, Gilbert Antoine de St. Maxent, who had already guessed the situation was irreversible.

The next governor, Luis de Unzaga, who later married my sister Isabel, was more tactful from the beginning than his predecessors had been in his dealings with the French Creoles, listening to their appeals and even trusting them with government positions. Someone had mentioned to me that Unzaga was about to be replaced by another Spanish officer, and I must confess that my curiosity was piqued. However, my curiosity was certainly not what was keeping me awake at night.

On a moonlit night, I left my room and started pacing across the veranda facing the river. Under the intense moonlit sky, the size of the Mississippi was breathtaking. The intense brightness illuminated the river banks that were thick with bulrushes and palm trees. But there was something almost stony about that huge, apparently unmoving mass, as if instead of the river's mouth I were contemplating an immense volcanic crater brimming with lava. Under the moon's sad, white shroud, the river's pageant evoked somber memories, such as the death of the first Spanish explorers at the hands of the upstream Indians. They targeted the conquistadors' cadavers to such an extent that Hernando de Soto's lifeless body had to be hidden in the trunk of a willow to prevent its desecration.

Despite the attempts of other European travelers who had ventured to journey up the river to try to control its course and re-direct its current, the river kept devouring land and crushing all living things in its path. We men and women who lived in the Mississippi Valley wanted to use its fertile banks to establish farms and plantations. We knew that when the "Father of Waters," who was so-called by the Indians, unleashed one of his unforeseen and violent floods, we were going to be dispossessed of our property and would have to take refuge on high ground or climb the trees rapidly, just as swarms of insects clung desperately to logs floating on the waters.

Recently, I found out that to elude the taxes Spanish customs collected, as they passed through New Orleans the English merchants living on the left bank of the Mississippi attempted to dig a channel from Lake Pontchartrain to the river by taking advantage of the lake's single outlet to the open sea. With the diligence and tenacity that the Anglo-Saxon people usually show when they are trying to elude a toll imposed by foreign authorities, a crew of military engineers forced a battalion of slaves to dig a vast trench to connect the river with the lake. But the English probably had not asked the Father of Waters for permission to carry out their project, because when the canal work was well advanced, the Mississippi let loose its flood waters on that trench and created a massive mudslide full of rocks and tree trunks originating in its headwaters. In a matter of seconds, the engineers saw their carefully prepared floodgates fly through the air and the river erect an immense barrier of detritus in the still unexcavated part of the canal they had been digging, which no human hand could dislodge.

Despite its unpredictable mood swings, we who live near the great river are proud to be that powerful monster's neighbors, but we always consider it a wild beast that can be caged but never completely tamed, capable of suddenly raging and taking the lives of men and animals in one blow. I have heard wonderful stories about the river from my old nurse, Mulinde, the daughter of a black slave and a young Indian captive. Through her veins runs the blood of African witchdoctors; their knowledge has merged in her consciousness with the traditions of the Mississippi-area Indians.

When, on that very night, I noticed that the dawn light was beginning to filter through the trees in the garden and I had yet to fall asleep, I got dressed. I went down to breakfast and asked one of the slaves to prepare a carriage for me so I could get to the plantation shacks where Mulinde lived. As on other occasions, I noted that when I entered her hut, the slave Mulinde already "knew" I was soon to arrive at the plantation as she had known on other occasions.

"Mademoiselle de St. Maxent," the slave said to me. She still called me by my maiden name, as if time and space had erased the years I was married. *"Je suis bien contente de vous voir, mais comment ça se fait que vous êtes ici tellement de bonne heure?"*

Although she feigned surprise at seeing me at the plantation so early, she had put on new flowery skirts and a fuchsia turban on her head; which was not the way she usually dressed to work in the tobacco-drying shed.

In the past, Mulinde had sometimes read my thoughts as if I were an open book. I knew that to be able to use her gifts of clairvoyance, she had to smoke a couple of pipes worth of herbs that when burned produced a sweet odor too strong for my taste. I sat down on a wooden stool under a sycamore tree, while the slave squatted in the sand, taking long puffs from her meerschaum pipe. Those herbs had not always had an immediate effect, but on that occasion Mulinde seemed to go into a trance quickly, and the words she mumbled burst forth oddly from her mouth, as if they had emanated from her without belonging to her.

"I understand Mademoiselle is nervous and even a little crazy, because doubtless you've guessed that very soon events will happen that will profoundly affect your future."

(This is my personal interpretation of her speech, which was hard for me to understand because Mulinde spoke some words in her mother's Indian dialect and other words in *patois creole*. In her delirium, her trembling lips also slurred the words.)

"I see a man who will arrive at the port in a few days, where many citizens and a great number of soldiers will congregate to welcome him. He's a man, not too tall, young but not very handsome, although I sense he has a great strength of character. I predict this man will occupy a very important place in Mademoiselle's life."

I did not want to interrupt her, but I thought to myself that Mulinde was mistaken about this, because I didn't yet consider myself ready to contemplate a serious relationship with another man.

"The man I see has been called upon to occupy important posts and will obtain great victories against his country's enemies. He will become a king or something similar in a place where there are great treasures of silver and gold. And if Mademoiselle accepts him as her husband, he will give you more children and make you very happy."

I noted that Mulinde suddenly fell silent, as if she were seeing a vision that was not as positive or as pleasant as the one she had just related to me.

After a long silence she said, "I sense the man has committed a terrible sin in the past and, if he wants to ease his conscience, he'll have to remedy his mistake or at least recognize it. I could not glimpse exactly what happened, but I am guessing the man will have to atone for that sin by performing a good deed. Otherwise, if he wants to live near the Father of Waters, that father will not accept him as one of his children and will send gales, downpours and storms against him."

CHAPTER 16
The Port of New Orleans
(Bernardo de Gálvez speaks)

The journey from El Ferrol to New Orleans, with a stop in Havana, seemed very brief, in part because we sailed with very favorable winds, but also because I was so absorbed in studying all the information about Louisiana that my uncle José had given me that I barely felt the thirty days aboard the ship go by. I understood that the responsibilities awaiting me would have been daunting for a less energetic and ambitious man than I. But meeting those responsibilities was a challenge I not only accepted but relished.

Given that my uncle was very concerned about commerce in our dominions, he had insisted that I adopt strict measures against shady trading and contraband. It would do Spain no good to have a customs house at the river's mouth at the port of New Orleans if along the entire length of the river, commerce was unregulated and, therefore, taxes were not paid. It seemed that my predecessors had ignored this problem to avoid upsetting our English neighbors living on the river's left bank. They were the ones controlling illegal trading with the Europeans as well as with the Indians, whom they had subdued by selling them arms and alcohol.

Perhaps the most immediate and important recommendation was to obtain information about what was happening in the English colonies in their struggle to free themselves from England. My uncle had authorized me to pay spies with money from the treasury and to spare no expense in obtaining information.

I was so absorbed in going over my papers, I had barely set foot on the ship's deck during the voyage, so that the morning we arrived at our destination, the captain had to come to my cabin to inform me we were nearing the river's mouth. Then, I put my pen down to take up the sword and put on the uniform of a colonel in the Louisiana Standing Regiment. It was customary for the new military commander to review the troops upon his arrival. Once I was attired in my dress uniform—blue waistcoat and breeches, red lapels and collar, and my shirt's gold buttons affixed—I went up to the Santa Catalina's bridge. The brigantine's prow was already plowing the estuary's waters through the keys covered in dense tropical vegetation, while straight ahead, I could see the port of New Orleans' skyline.

From the bridge, my eyes could barely encompass the panorama of the banks of the powerful river flowing swiftly towards the open sea. It was a flow of cinnamon-colored waters in which gigantic tree trunks, which had been upended somewhere upstream, were like pieces of carrot floating in a bowl of soup. I remembered then the map of the Mississippi my uncle had shown me the same morning he announced my appointment. Although the French engineer's map was beautifully and precisely drawn, the artist had not been able to capture on paper the majesty of the river's raw and unrestrained power.

As I contemplated that miracle of nature, I felt contradictory sensations arise in me. On the one hand, I had the pleasure of enjoying a grand and uniquely beautiful spectacle; on the other, as the Crown's representative charged with expanding Spain's authority over the entire length of the river, I knew that to carry out my mission I would have to subdue that powerful rival.

When at last I saw the soldiers of the Standing Regiment and the perfectly uniformed Creole militia by their side at the foot of the dock, I immediately forgot about my conflicting impulses. I could now indulge in the warm welcome given by the army and the citizens of New Orleans. As soon as I stepped off the boat, Governor Luis Unzaga approached, saluted and embraced me most cordially. Once I had reviewed the troops, Governor Unzaga indicated to me that the soldiers as well as the citizens were waiting for the new colonel and future governor to say a few words to inaugurate my command informally. I stepped up to a small dais, where other military officers and civic leaders sat, and hearing some comments in French over the din, I suddenly had the intuition to give my speech in French. So I did.

"Your Excellency, Governor Unzaga, military officers and civil authorities, ladies and gentlemen, I am Bernardo de Gálvez, appointed colonel of the Louisiana Standing Regiment by His Majesty the King of Spain. I judge this posting to be a great honor and I hope to carry out my duties with the zeal and dedication I have previously demonstrated in other positions in the service of His Majesty. I propose to better the quality of life in this territory and to secure the prosperity and happiness of all its residents."

I paused in my speech and looked around to observe the effect my words were having. At that very moment, I felt like someone was staring intently at me; although I could not imagine where that gaze was coming from.

"When I speak of everyone's happiness, it is because I think that in Louisiana there should be no difference between the citizens of French origin and those of Spanish origin. If there were such a difference, we would be betraying the wishes of His Majesty the Catholic King Charles III and his best friend and ally, the Catholic King of France. Both monarchs desire that the strong family ties that bind them together should also unite those of us here who share a common culture, religion and the pursuit of good fortune. Therefore, it is my wish to thank all of you for this heartfelt welcome that from this day forward I will always remember. I shall conclude my remarks by saying, 'Long live Spain and Long live France!'"

After I finished my speech, the crowd packing the port area, and especially the group of distinguished citizens seated on the dais, erupted in such thunderous applause that the entire fragile, wooden stage shook. Nevertheless, I still felt that same persistent gaze that had been following me from the moment I had set foot on land to receive the governor's embrace. While I was watching the troops parade, as well as during my speech, I had the sensation someone was closely observing my every move. I am not referring to the hundreds of eyes fixed on my person, but rather to a specific pair of eyes staring at me with intensity.

In the Book of John, it is told that once when a multitude was crowding around Jesus Christ, he turned to one of the disciples and said, "Who touched me? Someone touched me." The disciple answered him, "But Master, you are surrounded by a mass of people struggling to be near you to receive your blessing. How are we to know who has touched you?" But Jesus knew that his contact with that hand had been different. It turned out to be the hand of a mother who was confident the Master would heal her sick son. Just as in that passage of the Gospel, someone had bestowed upon me a special lingering stare among the crowds of men and women surrounding me. I guessed immediately that those eyes belonged to a woman, probably a beautiful woman.

CHAPTER 17
Aid to the Rebels

When the ceremony ended, Bernardo de Gálvez asked the outgoing governor to begin the transfer of power by accompanying him on board the brigantine.

"I'd like to congratulate you on your speech," Unzaga told him. "I think your words will go far in smoothing our relationship with our formerly French citizens, a situation other governors and I have had to handle despite some unpleasant turns. If I had known you were fluent in French, I myself would have recommended you speak in that language. Now, the majority of this colony's citizens speak French."

"I was lucky to spend time in a French military academy, where I learned many things besides the language," replied Gálvez, raising a glass of sherry to toast Unzaga before lunch was served in the colonel's cabin.

"It goes without saying that, for my part, I shall gladly provide you with all the information available on Louisiana. But before discussing those matters, I would like to comment on a subject I consider pressing, specifically your move to the city, since I assume this ship is soon to weigh anchor. I would have liked to put you up in my home, but the governor's residence, which was already not in great shape, has suffered damage in the recent hurricane and is in no condition to house anyone. When he found out about the situation, a New Orleans gentleman named Gilbert Antoine de St. Maxent, who has already rendered important services to Spain, offered his home to you. It is a place with ample space and well-endowed with all the amenities, you may stay there as long as you judge necessary."

"If you recommend it, I'll not question your advice. I'll lodge at Mr. St. Maxent's house. I had the pleasure of meeting him during the greeting ceremony that was so kindly prepared for me. This frigate must leave for Veracruz in a few days, but until I've gotten used to the climate and put my belongings in order, I'll remain on board, if you don't mind."

"Of course, it's just an offer, not an obligation. What I would recommend is for you to enjoy the dinner Mr. St. Maxent is holding in your honor tonight at his house. It will give you a chance to judge for yourself if you're interested in accepting his invitation to lodge there or not." The governor paused before adding with a smile, "Although you may judge for yourself his residence's suitability, if you accept his invitation tonight, you'll find that the gentleman has several daughters, including the young widow, Felicitas de St. Maxent, who is celebrated in the city as a woman of exceptional beauty and charm. Actually, all of her sisters are attractive young women," Unzaga added, his tanned, leathery cheeks blushing, "but the only one among St. Maxent's daughters you can't flirt with is María Isabel, whom I had the good fortune of marrying about a year ago."

"I accept St. Maxent's dinner invitation with pleasure and I won't let the opportunity to admire the young ladies' beauty slip by. I only ask you to come by for me at the dock at the appropriate time. And if you like, we can make time now to discuss several issues. I'd very much like to know your opinion, if you're willing to share it with me."

"Of course, I'd be happy to. Besides, it's my duty. As you've been in Madrid recently, I'm wondering if you've brought clear instructions concerning our English neighbors and the aid promised to the rebels, as well. I confess, perhaps because of my lack of direct contact with those in charge of these issues in the government, I don't have a clear picture of what Madrid wants us to do in New Orleans."

Perhaps emboldened by the two glasses of sherry he had downed on an almost empty stomach, Gálvez replied, "You could hardly have received specific instructions, when no one in Madrid has a clear idea of what to do about the situation. I beg you not to take my comments to be cavalier or inappropriate. If I may be candid, I'll tell you our policy on this conflict is highly ambiguous, if not contradictory."

"Indeed, I had the same impression. On the one hand, I received instructions to remain on good terms with our English neighbors. On the other, a few months ago, the captain general of Cuba sent me a load of gunpowder and other military supplies with a confidential note that I should turn it all over to agents of the rebel army who would be in touch with me about the delivery. To keep up public appearances, it occurred to me I should arrest the American captain who had come down to New Orleans to receive the supplies. Afterwards, I dispatched the barrels of gunpowder as if they were barrels of lard, among other supplies, so that it would appear to be a private commercial transaction and not a donation from the Spanish Crown. The rebel officer paid me with a letter of credit tendered by the House of Burgesses in the amount of one thousand eight hundred and fifty dollars in pieces of eight.

"I think that it's very important to document our exact military aid because it's the only way we'll recover our money at the end of the war."

"On the other hand, the same officer who had come to pick up those supplies gave me a letter written by General Charles Lee addressed to me, who, as you know, is one of George Washington's principal aides. In the letter, Lee asked for Spain's help, arguing that if the English were to win the war, the entire territory, including New Spain would be insecure. However, he stated, if the rebel colonies were to win their independence, Spain would have nothing to fear from the new country because the New Englanders, for several reasons, are only interested in commerce and agriculture and have no interest in territorial expansion."

Gálvez slowly savored the wine in his glass before replying. "You already know how that nation of farmers by fighting tooth and nail took over the territories the English Crown had reserved by treaty for the Indians who had helped them in the last war."

Well into the afternoon, Gálvez and Unzaga shared their experiences and insights on multiple topics. Only when the waters around the dock began reddening with the setting sun did the governor realize there was barely enough time for them to change clothes, leave the ship and hasten to the dinner given in honor of the new governor by Gilbert Antoine de St. Maxent.

CHAPTER 18
Those Eyes Leave an Impression

That very morning, Felicitas de St. Maxent had asked her father's permission to stay at home to rest and not to attend with the rest of the family the reception for Bernardo de Gálvez at the dock. Gilbert Antoine, who was already wearing his dress uniform of colonel of the Creole Militia, insisted she not miss such an important event. To fulfill her father's wishes, the young widow powdered her nose, sprayed herself with perfume, put on a garnet velvet gown and covered her head with a lacy Spanish mantilla. When she stepped unto the dais on her father's arm and took her place, where the military and civil authorities had gathered to receive the new governor, a hushed wave of admiration fell on the crowd.

After attending the ceremony at the New Orleans dock and shutting herself away in her room, Felicitas was overcome with an even greater anxiety than she had been feeling recently. Up until then, she had not been able to express why she felt so uneasy. But when she saw the new governor step off the launch with the red and white banner of St. Andrew at its stern, she felt a strong attraction to the stranger. What a sight to behold: Bernardo de Gálvez walking down the pier in his bright new uniform, the midday sun shining on his gold braid epaulettes and perfectly polished gold buttons. He drew and brandished his steel blade that glinted imposingly, as if he were the Greek god Triton clad in a tunic of shining scales, instead of an officer disembarking from an ocean voyage.

When she heard the officer's deep and well-modulated voice giving his speech in French, Felicitas shivered all over, especially when he said the French word "felicité" several times, which she interpreted as a premonition, although she could not say why. As she had tossed and turned in bed, Felicitas realized it was inappropriate for a young widow to feel such a strong attraction to a man she did not even know.

Felicitas wondered if Mulinde's prophecy might have steered Cupid's arrow by telling her she would meet a man who would find an important place in her heart. If that prediction turned out to be true, would it not also follow that the gentleman had committed a terrible sin in the past, a sin requiring him to redeem himself? The French have a proverb about first impressions that contradicts the traditional advice of not judging a book by its cover: *"Méfiez vous! C est la bonne!"* (Although it may not seem so, your first impression is always right!) The resolve and firm voice with which he had given his speech as he had reviewed the troops gave Felicitas the clear impression he was a man of noble character, incapable of committing a vicious act.

Because Felicitas served as lady of the house in her father's mansion, she had to interrupt her musing and get busy giving orders to the slaves and servants to prepare the meal her father was giving that evening to honor Bernardo de Gálvez. After donning a white muslin dress, which flattered her bronze skin, and a green satin bodice that matched her blue-green eyes, she went down to the salon to receive their guests, who murmured their approval. That was all she needed to sit down to dinner next to the stranger who had unexpectedly warmed her heart.

At the beginning, Felicitas took advantage of her role as hostess to engage each guest at the dinner table. Seated next to the guest of honor, Bernardo de Gálvez, not even the flapping of her fan, whose lacy fringes seemed to be about to take flight, saved her from having to look at the Spaniard directly and from conversing with him for a while. As soon as they exchanged glances, Bernardo had the feeling that the eyes that had observed him so intently from the second he set foot on the dock belonged to the lady seated at his side.

When Bernardo returned to his cabin, the memory of the lady's eyes peeking at him from behind her fan kept him awake. At that same moment, Felicitas was on her veranda looking out at the silhouette of the Spanish brigantine. Perhaps the perfumed night air carried her yearning to him, because Bernardo felt a tug on his heart strings and went up on deck again to enjoy the view of the estuary in the moonlight.

The ship rocked gently. Although the slow current could hardly be felt, Bernardo knew that the undertow was flowing at four to five knots below the apparently calm waters of the surface. The moon's muted glow emanating over the estuary gave the current a metallic, viscous appearance, which reminded him of the pond brimming with quicksilver he had seen at the Almadén mines.

CHAPTER 19
Oliver Pollock

Unzuaga had agreed to meet Gálvez again on board the frigate to continue discussing issues of common interest. When he returned to the ship the next morning, he was not alone in the long boat that had picked him up at the dock. He was accompanied by an awkward young man whose most distinguishing feature was his curly red locks and matching long sideburns. He remained on deck while the governor went down to Bernardo de Gálvez's cabin.

"Colonel Gálvez, I've taken the liberty of coming on board in the company of a friend I would like to present to you. I think he could prove very useful in dealing with the matter of the aid Madrid wishes to send to the rebel colonists. The Irishman's name is Oliver Pollock, a businessman and financier. His principal occupation now is acting as the unofficial representative of the American Congress in this city as they rasie funds for their cause of independence and secure supplies for the rebel troops.

"It seems that my interests may dovetail with the young Irishman's," said Gálvez.

"Pollock has succeeded in amassing a rather considerable fortune, which he is putting at the service of the revolution to throw the English out of its American colonies. He lives and breathes only to accomplish that. When he found out there was going to be a new governor of this province, he asked me to try to obtain an audience with you as soon as possible. Therefore, I have dared to bring him aboard your ship. But if you would prefer to postpone the meeting for another time, I've already told Pollock you and I have other urgent matters to attend to."

"On the contrary, I can think of nothing more urgent than meeting a friend of Spain and an enemy of England."

"Pollock is completely fluent in Spanish. He lived in Havana for a few years and has a great affinity for our culture and religion. If you would permit me a small indiscretion that could help you deal with this man, I'll tell you that the first time I told Pollock about your arrival in Louisiana, he warned me that if the future governor favored Great Britain, he would not stay in the city even twenty-four hours. If on the other hand the future governor was aligned with the French crown's position, then you would have at your service the most honest and capable businessman in all Louisiana."

When his aide informed Pollock he could enter the colonel's cabin, the Irishman entered and bowed deeply before the future governor and pronounced a few words of greeting. He then retrieved a letter from his jacket's inner pocket and gave it to Gálvez. The letter was signed by Patrick Henry, the governor of Virginia, and it was already translated into Spanish. In a rhetorical style not lacking a certain beauty, Henry began by acknowledging Spain as a great commercial power and went on to promise trade concessions with the newly independent nation, once Spain defeated its "old and natural enemy," England. Henry specified that once the United States won the war, the entire flow of commerce from the northern states would be funneled down the Mississippi River to New Orleans, with prosperity for the city as a result.

Gálvez thought about Henry's proposition for a while and realized it was a pretext for cutting back Spain's ability to collect customs taxes on the Mississippi River.

"I'll need to consult Madrid before answering Mr. Henry's letter, Mr. Pollock, but you can tell him that from now on the interests of Spain and the English colonies in facing our common enemy is leading us to consider all your proposals with great interest."

Oliver Pollock's ruddy face, with its nose covered in freckles that gave him a childish appearance, lit up with joy.

Gálvez wanted to capitalize on Pollock's enthusiasm by offering his guest something the Irishman was not expecting: "It's my understanding that the colonial troops fighting in the North need arms and ammunition sent to them, as well as medicine and warm clothing to withstand the brutal winter in those latitudes. Is that not so?"

Gálvez took a sheet of paper from a folder on his desk that listed products and read it aloud for dramatic effect.

"On this manifest given to me before I left El Ferrol are six boxes of quinine, one hundred bolts of heavy cloth, one hundred barrels of gunpowder and three hundred muskets with bayonets in thirty boxes. Do you, Mr. Pollock, believe these arms, medicine and cloth will be enough for the troops in the North?"

Pollock could not find the words to respond, but every freckle on his nose glowed with joy. "Perhaps by divine Providence the list of supplies you've just read corresponds exactly to what is so urgently needed in the northern forts in danger of being retaken by the enemy."

"Well, all of it is stowed in the hold of this very frigate. My only request is that you unload these boxes and packages discreetly and as soon as possible, as well as the barrels of gunpowder. I'm not happy about this brigantine continuing to be a traveling arsenal. The ship should be leaving for other destinations very soon. So forthwith, please have the cargo transported to whatever ship you designate, tonight if possible."

Deeply moved, Pollock wept as he took the colonel's hand between his and squeezed it for a long time, wetting their hands with his tears of joy.

CHAPTER 20
Skirmishes on Different Battlefields

Until Gálvez could evaluate the situation and weigh the balance of power during the first months after his arrival, he decided to respect the status quo on the border with the English and even became friendly with the governor of Pensacola, Peter Chester, by sending him several cases of Malaga wine and tobacco rolls from the Havana drying sheds. However, he was fully aware that the English merchants had abused the good graces of the previous Spanish governors by turning the shores of the great river into a nest of smugglers and pirates. The English only had the right of navigation on the river but not of commerce. Nevertheless, their brazen black-marketeering had gotten to such a point that they had even built pontoons for docking in plain sight. Although Gálvez appeared to have accepted the situation, he was only waiting for an excuse to implement the drastic measures he had proposed from the first day of his arrival.

The West Florida, an English frigate, had seized three Spanish ships on Lake Pontchartrain unannounced: a schooner and two barges working in the extraction of pitch destined for shipyard in Cuba. Gálvez finally had the excuse he was waiting for and gave orders for the gunboats patrolling the river to embargo eleven English vessels used for contraband and escort them to New Orleans to be charged with piracy. Gálvez also issued an edict ordering all English subjects to abandon Spanish Louisiana Territory within two weeks.

When Pensacola Governor Chester was informed of Gálvez's edict, he immediately sent the frigate Atlanta, under the command of Captain Thomas Lloyd, to New Orleans. When the English ship arrived at the port of New Orleans and aimed its cannons at the city, Lloyd sent Gálvez a letter demanding an explanation for what he termed Gálvez's "extraordinary conduct," which countervened the 1763 Treaty of Paris guaranteeing the right of English ships to navigate the Mississippi.

Gálvez was perfectly aware of the risk he was taking. The palisade protecting New Orleans and the San Juan Bayou on the other side of the river was rotted away from the humidity and its cannons, continuously exposed to the elements, had completely rusted. But he would not be intimidated by the presence of the man o'war or by Captain Lloyd's arrogant words. He responded to Lloyd's letter politely but very firmly. Gálvez observed that the right of way on the Mississippi did not authorize English ships to carry contraband. On the other hand, he reminded the English captain that the ship under his command had intimidated with cannon fire the French ship Marguerite and the Spanish ship María and detained them in Gulf waters for no apparent reason. Lloyd responded that he had done so believing they were pirates.

After the exchange of letters, the confrontation came to naught, when English merchants themselves, who had been forced out of Louisiana, defended the Spanish governor's conduct. The British frigate had no choice but to turn around and head back to Pensacola.

When Gálvez informed the Governor of Cuba, Diego Navarro, about the incident, Gálvez boasted about "having received the English with cannon fuses lit." But he knew full well that if he had been forced to light the fuses for combat, the city's fortifications would not have withstood the English ship's first volley. Gálvez asked Navarro for naval as well as troop reinforcements. Governor Navarro understood New Orleans was at risk and sent the frigate Volante to the port city. But in responding to Gálvez's letter, he took the opportunity to include a stiff reprimand for his reckless behavior, reminding him that the Spanish government had not changed their instructions and that he was to appease the English.

Don José de Gálvez found out about the incident and considered it the first feint in a duel that both countries considered to be inevitable. He did not hesitate to support his nephew and gave instructions to Governor Navarro to make more ships available, just in case, and gave him orders to send reinforcements to Gálvez's standing battalion. Don José even mentioned to the King what had happened and later wrote to Bernardo that His Majesty had approved of the firmness of his actions in that situation. This was indeed support at the highest level for Bernardo's decisions, that others had judged to be reckless. This difference of opinion between the Crown and the governor of Cuba, who was the military commander upon whom Gálvez depended, would not benefit Gálvez's projects in the long run.

The Lake Pontchartrain incident, as well as Gálvez's support for the revolutionary army forts in the upper Mississippi, was noticed in the British capital. In response, the English Commander-in-Chief, Henry Clinton, decided to reinforce the garrisons in Bute (Manchac), Panmure (Natchez) and Baton Rouge, and he sent Brigadier General John Campbell, who up until then had been fighting in the North, to Pensacola. Likewise, he sent troops from Waldeck's German and American Royalist units from Pennsylvania and Maryland to the garrisons defending Mobile and Pensacola. Although Gálvez could have interpreted Clinton's actions to be defensive, he concluded that the English had already been preparing an attack on Louisiana, so he sped up his preparations to improve New Orleans' defenses.

In the meanwhile, on the chess board of European politics, the pieces were also in motion. The French Foreign Minister, the Count of Vergennes, had succeeded in persuading King Louis XVI to recognize the independence of the English colonies in North America, which in practice meant the outbreak of hostilities with England. Charles III had no choice but to follow the French initiative, begrudgingly, and he sent an ultimatum to London. Any negative response from King George III would amount to a declaration of war. But clinging to his biases on the subject of colonial revolution, the Catholic King would not send an expeditionary force to fight alongside the Continental Army or recognize, at least for the moment, the new country's independence.

Although the war with England was going to affect other territories in the Americas, as the Secretary for the Indies José de Gálvez had predicted when he sent his nephew to Louisiana, the war's first skirmishes were going to be unleashed on the banks of the Mississippi River. Fortunately, Bernardo de Gálvez had anticipated the outbreak of hostilities by expelling the territory's English neighbors from the river basin and preparing the standing regiment and the Creole militia for combat.

Bernardo de Gálvez' thoughts, however, were not only concerned with the military. He knew that by accepting lodging in the home of Gilbert Antoine de St. Maxent and his beautiful daughters he had opened an unforeseen battle front in his personal life. Felicitas tried to hide her infatuation from Bernardo by employing the typical feminine wiles. The best proof of her feelings was when she saw him on the dock's esplanade and in speaking to him feigned disdain or indifference. Bernardo noticed that when he got close to any of her sisters, Felicitas shooed them away, which meant that she had targeted him.

Living under the same roof had fostered Felicitas' and Bernardo's relationship, but it had also complicated it. For a time, each kept a formal distance from the other so as not to betray the trust St. Maxent had extended to the stranger on offering him lodging in his own home.

CHAPTER 21
Complicated Living Arrangements
(Felicitas St. Maxent speaks)

I am wholly convinced that my father, who is a total gentleman, could not have imagined that, after having worn widow's weeds for my deceased husband for more than two years, I had fallen head over heels in love with a man I barely knew. But, unfortunately, not all the city's denizens are equally as chivalrous or trusting as my father. Surely, a matron somewhere is scandalized a single young man is living under the same roof as a widow and three young women of marriageable age.

To avoid tongues wagging and despite observing good manners according to the basic rules of hospitality, I've decided to behave coldly around our illustrious guest. However, I trust that, given Bernardo's keen sensibilities, it cannot have escaped him that I do not treat my friends, my father's friends or our family members, or even my own servants and slaves in the cold and unpleasant way I address him. Indeed, it is a rare day I do not find a bouquet of flowers that the Spaniard has gathered for me from the garden flowerbeds and sent with a thoughtful note, delivered by one of the female slaves to my rooms. I hope these kindnesses on his part are not merely a hunter's ploy, a means to carve yet another notch on his bedpost.

I understand perfectly well that Bernardo cannot spend too much time on our relationship. He took over a less than desirable situation. If the English decide to attack New Orleans, the city does not have adequate defenses or enough troops, even if we add my father's militias to the Standing Regiment, to repulse the double threat of the mighty British naval fleet and its army. Despite the situation, Bernardo's spirits have not flagged. He comes to the dining room every morning to eat breakfast with the family and has a merry spark in his eyes, really a sly twinkle that melts my heart.

Because our guest's rooms are not far from my bedroom, I found out a secret dispatch from the Madrid government had arrived on a Spanish ship. The letter told him Spain was just about ready to declare war on England, but because he was not interested in divulging the news until the right time, Bernardo only met in private with army and militia commanders and two senior officials in the New Orleans civil administration. I heard them talking at the war council that met in our dining room. Because my father did not want any servant entering the chamber, it fell to me to serve the hot chocolate and cakes.

Bernardo explained the situation succinctly. While the regular English and German troops were eight hundred rifles strong, without counting the Indian auxiliary troops and the citizens loyal to the British crown, the Spanish garrison had fewer than six hundred men. Of these, two thirds were insufficiently trained militiamen and young recruits. To compensate for our side's disadvantage, Bernardo proposed using the element of surprise and taking the offensive. When I overheard all of this, I felt embarrassed by my compatriots' cowardice: the greater part of those present—with the exception of my own father and the Irishman Oliver Pollock—declared themselves absolutely against attacking the English until the reinforcements requested from Havana arrived in New Orleans. Some of those gathered around the table hesitated to express their opinions and merely sunk their noses into their cups of hot chocolate.

CHAPTER 22
The Father of Waters Strikes

(Felicitas de St. Maxent continues speaking)

Given his civil and military aides' hesitance, Bernardo sought support for his campaign in the flotilla of barges plying the Mississippi, among the peddlers who sold their wares at port, among the Indians who came down the river to sell hides and even among the slaves who had escaped from the British yoke seeking better treatment under the Spanish Crown. Making the best of a bad situation, Bernardo succeeded in arming the ships and gathering a militia that, despite the recruits' raw inexperience, was ready to take on the seasoned "Red Coats" and risk putting themselves within reach of Indian tomahawks.

The Father of Waters, however, had not given his blessing to Bernardo's plans. When everything was ready, clouds so dark they seemed to have spewed from Hell suddenly gathered over the Mississippi. With a terrifying crashing of thunder and lightning bolts, the Heavens unleashed a downpour of such magnitude that in a matter of hours the river had overflowed, smashing the ships moored at the docks against its banks, flooding the militia's barracks, carrying away arms and munitions and destroying the crops intended to supply food to the troops.

I was caught in the downpour while taking a walk through the city. The wind wrenched my parasol from my hands, and I ran to find refuge in a shed to wait for the storm to let up. There I remembered Mulinde's vision and it occurred to me that the Father of Waters had just delivered a mighty blow against the governor's plans. When I managed to get home completely soaked, the servants told me Bernardo had left as soon as the rain had started to come down. I lay awake for a long time in my bedroom and fell asleep without hearing Bernardo return to his room. Later, I found out that he had been visiting the places most affected by the storm throughout the night, attempting to bail water from the ships and trying to estimate the personal and material damage the flood had inflicted.

As soon as the sun's first rays peeked out from among the still stormy clouds, I jumped out of bed and asked one of the slaves to saddle my mare so I could ride to the plantation where Mulinde worked. To get there, I had to leave the river bank and go around the lowlands because they were all flooded. When I arrived, I saw that the high winds had torn the roofs off the slaves' quarters. Mulinde, as always, had sensed my arrival and was waiting for me, sitting on a sandy patch at the foot of a large sycamore tree and smoking her pipe of foul-smelling herbs.

As soon as she saw me dismount, the slave scolded me: "You can't say I didn't warn you! Although we're not yet in hurricane season, that man has caused the great river's curse to fall upon all of us. As much as I regret what happened, I'm glad you know I was not wrong when I told you that man drags a terrible sin behind him."

"Can't you recommend he do something to redeem himself? Possibly, you weren't wrong when you told me I would feel attracted to a certain gentleman, but how can I accuse someone I barely know of a sin I know nothing about or even when it happened?"

"You probably know what you're doing, Miss Felicitas, but if the Father of Waters continues to sulk because of that man's presence, he'll end up destroying our crops and drowning our people. It's already happened before in the deluge the friar told us about at the mission."

"If you could at least see in your dreams what his offense was or what sin he committed before he came here . . . "

Mulinde inhaled deeply from her pipe and threw bones on a patch of moist sand. After remaining silent a long while with her eyes closed, she whispered in her pidgin language, "The evening before last, on the eve of the downpour, I had a dream that could be related to my earlier vision. It's not easy to explain it because the dream happened in a very dark place, as if it were a cave or underground passage. I saw the shadow of a young man entering one of those forges where metals are melted. Other people carrying lanterns in their hands to light the way through the earth's bowels accompanied the young man until they arrived at a larger chamber, where he greeted another older man, whom I couldn't see clearly, although he gave me the impression he was extremely ill."

Mulinde, who always spoke with her eyelids half closed, opened her eyes wide for a moment to see the impression her words were having on me and then went on. "Next, the dream continued in another place, where there were statues of Christian saints on the walls. The old man gave the young man something wrapped in a tarry cloth, and the young man thanked him for it. Then I was shocked to see that the same men who had accompanied the young man to the underground cave had hidden behind some columns. One of them gestured, jerking his index finger across his neck, as if indicating that they intended to cut someone's throat."

Mulinde closed her eyes again, but her whole body shivered. "When I left the shack that same morning, I saw storm clouds gathering over the river and sensed the Father of Waters was going to show his indignation because of that murder."

CHAPTER 23
A Well-Placed Exhortation

Although the storm's destruction had dealt a severe blow to his campaign preparations, the new governor held his head high despite the adversity. Sure that his men had been ready to follow him, he concentrated on raising the troops' and the militiamen's morale before the deluge could dampen their fighting spirit. Bernardo understood that it was the right time to disclose the declaration of war he had received in the same dispatch that officially confirmed him as governor. Up until then he had kept it to himself, but now his keen political instincts told him it was the right time for the announcement.

With the help of a town crier, he ordered the troops of the standing regiment and the companies of black and mixed-race soldiers, who had already arrived from Havana and from New Spain, to gather in the main square of New Orleans. He also summoned the citizens who were shoveling mud from the streets or fixing the roofs of their houses, blown off by the strong winds. From one of the town hall's balconies, he spoke to the public, this time in Spanish without the resonance of his first speech, but nevertheless in a reassuring, firm tone:

"His Majesty's decree has just arrived with my official appointment as governor of Louisiana. But I cannot assume the office before swearing to defend the province. Although I am ready to shed my last drop of blood for Louisiana and for my King, I cannot swear an oath I may have to break without knowing first if you are ready to resist the brash designs of the English." Gálvez paused briefly to take in the crowd's reaction before adding, "What say you? Should I be sworn in as governor? Should I swear to defend Louisiana?"

One of the citizens in the town square stood up from his seat on a dilapidated cart whose wheels were stuck in the mud and spontaneously expressed the feelings of many in the crowd: "Swear to defend Louisiana and the King. We offer you our lives and our worldly goods, if anything is left after the storm."

Governor Bernardo de Gálvez once again saw that he had the support of the people.

Then, with the help of barge workers and fishermen, he proceeded to recover the four ships that flood waters had sent to the bottom of the river. He had them armed with light cannon and enabled them to navigate along the river bank as protection for the land expedition he himself was going to lead. On a hot August afternoon, when the humidity produced by the recent storm still hung in the air, a motley army of some seven hundred men, only a third of whom were seasoned soldiers, began ascending the river's left bank. His army consisted of recently arrived recruits from Mexico, local militiamen, companies of black and mixed-race free men eager to take revenge on their former owners; there was also a small group of American volunteers, among whom Oliver Pollock stood out for his revolutionary fervor.

Since a good portion of their arms and supplies had been lost during the storm, the troops had to arrive quickly at their destination in order to confiscate provisions from the English forts they would attack. For the next two weeks, the foot soldiers crossed dense forests and forded marches of waist-high water, after which they found clusters of leeches clinging to their calves.

As the army approached Fort Bute in Manchac, their first objective, the soldiers uniforms were wet and ragged, and many of the men were barefoot after having left their boots stuck in the mud. When Governor Gálvez checked on his troops, he verified that almost half of the men who had left New Orleans had succumbed to fever or had been lost in the jungle.

To attack the English fort successfully, Gálvez was counting on valuable information Gilbert Antoine de St. Maxent had gathered years before; St. Maxent's intelligence also included its artillery placement, as well as the number of officers and soldiers. The English had allowed St. Maxent, who for years had provided jerky and other foodstuffs to the soldiers, to operate freely in their strongholds. Fortunately, the news that war was declared had not yet reached Fort Bute and other isolated forts. Suddenly, Bute's officers looked on in terror as a loud company of dragoons, with bayonets fixed and ready for hand-to-hand combat, approached. After putting up a token resistance for the sake of British pride, Fort Bute surrendered at dawn the next day, but only after some soldiers had escaped through the surrounding underbrush. Gálvez's troops took two officers and eighteen soldiers prisoner that day.

Fort Baton Rouge, which was the next objective, proved somewhat tougher. A wide and deep moat encircled a steep wall with thirteen cannons in place to defend it. The fort enclosed a complement of four hundred regular soldiers and one hundred and fifty civilians, all loyal to the British crown. Using a tactic he had learned at the French military school, Gálvez created a diversion by cutting down trees and digging on the other side of the fort, as if his army were preparing to dig trenches there, but under the cover of night they set up their batteries directly across from the fort. When the cannons began to roar before dawn from the last place anyone was expecting, the English soldiers exited the fort bearing a white flag of truce.

Fort Baton Rouge's commander, Lt. Colonel Alexander Dickson, was forced to accept Governor Bernardo de Gálvez's stiff terms of unconditional surrender in addition to handing over Fort Panmure, which was protecting the city of Natchez. Gálvez had already dispatched a squad of militiamen under the command of Colonel St. Maxent to that city. However, the news of Dickson's surrender of two forts reached Brigadier General John Campbell in Pensacola in time for him to react. He quickly sent instructions to Captain James Foster, the commander of Fort Panmure, not to surrender but to resist the Spanish takeover. There, the English were counting on the support of numerous troops of Indians, whose faces were painted green, red, sometimes even with real blood, and whose war whoops took more of a toll on the enemy's morale than the tomahawks did on their bodies.

St. Maxent was the first to look out from the fort stockade peep hole at the risk of losing life and limb, or at least his scalp. On the other side of the stockade, the Indians were waiting.

Despite the show of British and Indian resistance, Oliver Pollock was able to send a courier to the citizens of Natchez, who, having changed citizenship various times during the last ten years, were not sufficiently loyal to the British to die defending them. He appealed to them by promising them advantages in their future business relations with Spain. The Irishman's letter was idealistic but practical and fulfilled its purpose: the local militias withdrew their support for Foster, forcing him to surrender his flag and eighty British army grenadiers.

A few days later, Bernardo de Gálvez would hear of the less-than-gallant behavior of the man who would be his rival when he attacked Pensacola. Initially, Brigadier General John Campbell had not believed the reports of Gálvez's military victories on the Mississippi, attributing them to the Spanish officer's strategy to force him to send reinforcements from Pensacola. But when he confirmed they were accurate, he attempted to exonerate himself for the defeat by sending a letter to the secretary for American affairs in London, Lord George Germain. In it, he assured him that the Spaniards had been preparing for war for a long time, which was true in part, and that American independence had been publicly proclaimed with pomp and circumstance in the streets of New Orleans, which was absolutely false.

When news of the surrender of the English forts on the Mississippi reached the Commander-in-Chief of the Continental Army George Washington, he celebrated the fact that Spanish arms had paralyzed every possible British attempt to control the Mississippi from the Gulf of Mexico northward. Because of those victories, Choctaw warriors upstream, who had been allies of the English until then, accepted an alliance with Spain; the Spaniards had turned out to be more powerful friends.

When Governor Bernardo de Gálvez returned to New Orleans, with a goodly cargo of foodstuffs and arms seized from the English, which replaced what had been lost during the Mississippi's flooding, the people received him enthusiastically, more for alleviating their hunger than for his military victories.

On returning home to the St. Maxent residence, Bernardo discovered Felicitas was throwing a party to celebrate his return and his victory over the English. The widow and her other sisters had donned their finest gowns for the occasion. After everyone dined on exquisite French cuisine and the best Bordeaux wines, which St. Maxent had been saving in his cellar for a special occasion, the band struck up the music. As befit the occasion, the guest of honor escorted Felicitas to the dance floor for the first waltz. It was the first time that Bernardo felt the beautiful widow's heart beat next to his, communicating with her body heat what her lips had not yet expressed. The governor and the widow did not care that the next day the rumor spread throughout the city that a romance was blossoming between them because they had danced in each other's arms until dawn.

CHAPTER 24
General Campbell's Letter
(Oliver Pollock speaks)

On my return from a trip to Philadelphia, I found out that the members of Congress were thankful that the shipment of arms and medicine upriver had saved Fort Kalaskia and Fort Vincennes for the Revolution. I had barely arrived in New Orleans, when I received a note from Governor Gálvez asking me to come by his office as soon as possible. So I left for headquarters without even stopping to change my clothes.

I had won over Spanish Governor O'Reilly and maintained a good relationship with him by selling his citizens flour at half the market price during a famine. I also secured Governor Unzaga's good will, and Gálvez treated me from the day of his arrival with such deference that I developed a special liking for him. I hope the new governor knows that I accepted the mission he entrusted to me because of my regard for him, even though it was not easy to carry out.

I had barely entered in his office when Gálvez gave me a letter and asked me to read it aloud. It was a letter addressed by General Campbell in Pensacola to the commander-in-chief of the English army, General Clinton. The letter had been intercepted by men from a Spanish vessel who had boarded an English packet boat. It read as follows:

Dear Sir,

With the official dispatches now in your hands, you may surely judge the unpleasant situation we find ourselves in here. I am fully confident this letter will succeed in convincing Your

Excellency to send the reinforcements you judge appropriate as soon as possible. On the other hand, you may completely rely on me to do everything in my power to defend
to my last breath our positions against any weapons Don
Gálvez may throw at our forts.

Therefore, I humbly ask you and I beg Your Excellency
be so kind as to reinforce the town with sufficient troops.
And if it cannot be so, to allow me to ask Your Excellency's
permission to seek another army posting instead of remaining here without the remotest possibility of serving rep-
utably and with honor and benefit for my lord the King.

"What do you think of this letter?" the governor asked me when
I finished reading it. The first thing that comes to mind is that my
English colleague in Pensacola isn't too enthusiastic about the day
we test the mettle of our forces in the siege of his town. But the most
interesting thing is that General Campbell recognizes the town does-
n't have enough men to assure victory."

"Indeed, Your Excellency, it's unheard of for General Campbell to
propose to his superior that he abandon the town if he can't reinforce
his troops. That could easily be considered an act of cowardice."

Gálvez smiled slightly as he watched me closely to observe my
reaction while he made the following proposal: "We are in agreement, but the reason I'm showing you the letter, Pollock, my friend,
is to help me find out exactly the condition of their defenses and
above all the English artillery's exact position and its firepower
around Pensacola. You may possibly be the only person I can trust
to carry out this mission. I'm telling you the truth here. I myself consider it extremely difficult and risky."

"Your Excellency knows I am willing to do anything you consider useful to assure the defeat of our common enemy."

I had hardly spoken those words, when I regretted having made
such a brash statement, especially when the Governor explained,
"Since General Campbell is probably unaware the letter never
reached Clinton's hands, perhaps we ourselves have the opportunity
to answer Campbell's letter any way we choose." Gálvez remained

silent for a few seconds as if to give me time to process the idea and then added, "Pollock, you're to carry a letter that is supposedly written by the English commander-in-chief in response to what his subordinate, General Campbell, has proposed."

I searched my mind for a few seconds before finding a valid reason to attempt to forego this mission. "With all due respect, Your Excellency, I must express my doubts about the viability of your strategy. Perhaps we can create confusion in the enemy's mind, but I think the deception will quickly be revealed."

By the grim tone with which he answered me, I understood Gálvez was not willing to free me from my commitment. "After the fact, I won't care a whit if the letter is found to be counterfeit. I'm only interested in having you find out the true condition of their defenses, the exact number of their defenders and the placement of their artillery . . . the letter will be a pretext to find these things out."

It had taken me some time to understand what the governor was proposing, and I was horrified once Gálvez showed me the letter addressed to Clinton. But I could not turn him down. I just nodded my head in agreement, put Campbell's letter in my pocket and asked the governor's permission to withdraw.

Gálvez's face had lit up with a smile when he knew I was ready to risk my life on his mission. Before letting me leave, he opened a drawer in his desk and took out a bottle carefully wrapped in a fine velvet bag and handed it to me.

"Pollock, I think Campbell will be more inclined to receive you if you present him with this small token of very old French cognac. According to my information, it's the general's favorite, despite the British being currently at war with France. Smiling, he added, "I suggest you not tell him it's from me."

After I left headquarters, I wandered around the docks for a while, in no particular direction. The more I thought about it, the more I became convinced that the mission was unfeasible because, although the letter might fool General Campbell and his aides, someone visiting Pensacola might recognize me. If I were discovered, the punishment for an act of espionage of this magnitude would be death.

Part Three

CHAPTER 25
In the Monastery Cloister
(Bernardo de Gálvez speaks)

In addition to the difficulties in recruiting enough men and obtaining arms and supplies to attack the fortified towns of Mobile and Pensacola, I was concerned about beginning a romantic relationship with Felicitas de St. Maxent. To avoid having people gossip about us, I moved out of Gilbert Antoine de St. Maxent's home, but not into the governor's mansion. Although Unzaga had already moved out of the residence, it needed repairs after the storm. Therefore, I had to accept the hospitality of the Capuchin monks, whose monastery was built of a much stronger material than most of the buildings in New Orleans. The monastery prior, Friar René Lambert, offered me a very spacious cell and the use of the chapter house for meetings with my aides. After eating breakfast in the refectory, I'd go stretch my legs strolling around the monastery's cloister with the prior, who spoke Catalan and understood Spanish because he was from Provence, France.

The monk had probably guessed that I was disinterested in the practice of my religion. One morning he said, "I've noticed, in the time you've lived among us, that Your Excellency does not often receive the sacraments. You haven't taken Holy Communion during Mass and, as far as I know, you haven't approached the confessional."

Taken aback by his candor, I answered, just as candidly, "Reverend, it's true that, although I'm a believer, I'm not much of a practicing Catholic. I think distancing myself a bit from religion has something to do with the years I spent in France at the military academy, where my companions lent me books by Rousseau and Voltaire.

Those readings made me understand my relationship with the Supreme Being differently."

"Well, I see that once again the Spaniards blame everything bad that happens on the French!" he said, laughing. "If I have taken the liberty of mentioning the necessity of getting closer to the Lord through the sacraments," he added more seriously, "it's because I think in troubled times like the ones you are going through, you need not only Divine intervention, but also the understanding and the affection of another human being to bring your desires and projects to fruition."

I stopped our promenade for a moment and looked hard at Lambert, imagining what he was going to say.

"I beg you not to take what I'm about to say as meddling or as indiscreet," he ventured, "but all New Orleans knows you are courting the daughter of Gilbert Antoine de St. Maxent, the beautiful Felicitas. I guess that for you this relationship must be, on the one hand, a source of satisfaction and joy and, on the other, a reason to worry. . . . "

"I would be lying if I said anything else. I confess that it surprises me that you've been able to read my mind so thoroughly. Are my thoughts written on my forehead?"

"Not at all . . . although your affable and open character leads you to express yourself in a good-natured way, my knowledge of the human soul has made me guess what's in your heart."

"All I can say is . . . I would like to satisfy the love I feel for Felicitas by asking her to marry me. Well, because . . . I'll never find another woman who has her combination of beauty, intelligence and charm. But there's an obstacle that won't be easy to overcome. As a high colonial official, I have to ask for royal permission to marry a woman from this colony."

"I know that's true, because the last governor had to request it before he could marry Isabel, Felicitas' sister. Is there some reason you can't do the same?"

"I'm afraid that . . . under normal circumstances it could take months to receive Madrid's authorization. But in a state of war, as is our present situation, this type of permission could take years to be granted."

"If you, Governor, were to leave here to do battle with the English—and it's possible your military posting will take you down other roads and to other lands—you will have done irrevocable harm to a woman who loves you." The prior paused briefly before adding, "I hope you will forgive my bluntness, but don't you think there can be an exception to the rule?"

"An exception to asking for royal permission? Impossible!"

"I know that another Spanish officer married a Louisiana citizen without asking for permission by celebrating the wedding *in articulo mortis*, in danger of dying"

I confess I was so astonished by the possibility that I didn't know what to say.

CHAPTER 26
The Father of Waters Strikes Again

There was quite a delay in the Havana military authorities sending the ships, troops and supplies that Bernardo de Gálvez had asked
for at the beginning of January 1780. Gálvez decided to gather the
troops he already had and transport them on his few available ships to
attack Fort Mobile, making a show of taking the town and thus
encouraging Cuba to help him to launch an attack on Pensacola. But
during yet another storm, his transport ships ran aground on a newly
formed sand bar at the river's mouth. Gálvez ordered the ships light-
ened, and the crews succeeded in rowing to the open sea, where the
Father of Waters brought a strong tide that scattered the vessels and
smashed six of them on the reefs.

When the storm had finally passed, Gálvez succeeded in refloat-
ing some of vessels and used some of the cannons from the wrecked
ships to set up a battery close to Fort Charlotte, the fort protecting the
entrance to Mobile Bay. Once the Spaniards were in position to attack
the city, Commander Elias Durnford of Mobile and Governor Gálvez
exchanged several letters to set the campaign's rules of engagement,
as was the custom between gentlemen. The English commander greeted Gálvez's messenger warmly at a banquet, where all the officers got
drunk toasting George III of England and Charles III of Spain.
Despite the camaraderie, they did not agree to a cease-fire. A few days
later, Durnford gifted Gálvez with twelve bottles of wine, a dozen
chickens, a ram and fresh bread; Gálvez reciprocated by sending him
a case of Bordeaux wine, another of Spanish wine, a few baskets of
oranges and a box of Cuban cigars.

Shortly thereafter, Gálvez chastised Durnford in a letter for destroying part of the city's outskirts in order to defend the fort: "Your forts were built to defend the people, but you are beginning to destroy the city in favor of the fort, which you are unable to defend."

While the warring leaders continued their banter, the Spaniards intercepted an English letter that revealed the besieged town of Mobile would be receiving reinforcements from Pensacola. That same evening, Gálvez decided to take action, giving instructions for his men to dig a trench from which they would bombard the enemy fort and for the Spanish ships to maneuver into the bay at dawn. In the wee hours of the morning, the Spaniards subjected the fort to a barrage from land and from the bay. It only took a couple of hours for Durnford to send an emissary proposing a cease-fire and surrender. Gálvez rejected the English commandant's first proposal to surrender the fort on the condition that his troops be allowed to depart for Pensacola but acceded to his second proposal that the garrison be taken prisoner, although the English soldiers would be allowed to receive war honors.

A little later, it was discovered that troops numbering nearly one thousand had departed from Pensacola for Mobile. But when the English commandant heard about the surrender of Fort Charlotte, he returned with his army to Pensacola. After parading to the beat of their drummers and with their rifles shouldered, the English surrendered their arms, and Gálvez took possession of the fort. He took more than two hundred prisoners of war. Once he was back in New Orleans, the cheering crowd carried Gálvez on their shoulders to the Capuchin monastery, where the governor had previously addressed them from the balcony.

After the festivities, Gálvez was alone with the prior.

In the monk's eyes there was a malicious glint. "You've done it, you've done it," said Reverend René Lambert.

"We've done it!"

"It's true, we've taken Mobile, but the hardest part is still ahead of us: the taking of Pensacola."

"Forgive me, but I wasn't referring to that," said the monk. "I'm so happy that I haven't made myself clear. I've taken the liberty of speaking with Felicitas, and she would be willing to marry you by celebrating the wedding ceremony *in articulo mortis.*"

Surprised, Gálvez managed to say, "I assume that to celebrate the ceremony, the circumstances have to be right, which is to say, either the bride or the groom should be at death's door."

The prior burst into one of his fits of laughter, which Gálvez did not find funny at all in that moment.

"Well, leave that to me. If you let me perform the ceremony, you won't have to worry. I'm not going to ask for a medical report."

CHAPTER 27
Cuban Molasses

Long before the American Revolutionary War, José de Gálvez had sent instructions to the governor of Havana to establish a network of spies throughout the Caribbean and to have them report directly to him what was happening in the conflict between England and its colonies.

He sent Luciano Herrera to Haiti, Florida merchant Egidio de Lapuente from Havana to Florida and Juan Miralles to Philadelphia. Miralles was Cuban Governor Diego José Navarro's brother-in-law.

Although many disparaged Miralles for his unsavory past as a smuggler and slave trader and some even accused him of having been in cahoots with the English when they captured Havana in 1762, he excelled in his duties as the Spanish Crown's unofficial agent to the English colonies, with which the Spanish Crown had no official diplomatic relations. Miralles' success was facilitated by his business relationship with Robert Morris, the American Revolution's most important financial backer, a relationship that had developed when Havana had been under English control. He had also collaborated with Oliver Pollock during that time.

Since Miralles had set up housekeeping in Philadelphia a month before M. Conrad Alexander Gerard, the French ambassador to the United States, arrived, the revolutionary congress had considered them to be equals, despite the fact that Miralles' only credentials were a letter of recommendation from Diego Navarro. Soon after arriving in Philadelphia, Miralles gave a magnificent banquet in honor of General Washington and his wife Martha. Washington knew perfectly well that the agent did not officially represent the Spanish Crown, but the general guessed that treating the Spanish commissioner generously would cultivate Spanish support for the Revolution. Curiously, the Count of Aranda also lead the French authorities to believe that Miralles had a mandate from the Spanish Crown, although he knew full well that Miralles was only an agent of the governor de Cuba.

Since supporting the Revolution did not prevent them from serving their own interests, Miralles' and Morris' schooners re-established their commercial exchange in the southern ports of the colonies and Cuba. Their ships transported a variety of products to Havana, such as rice and sugar, and returned via New Orleans loaded with military supplies, clothing and medicine. From New Orleans, Bernardo de Gálvez channeled them up the Mississippi River to the American rebels.

In March 1778, Miralles sent Oliver Pollock a donation of 3,000 yards of blue cloth, 6,000 yards of dyed, woolen cloth from the Alcoy factories, as well as six crates of quinine, eight crates of other medicines, 100 hundredweights of gunpowder in 100 barrels and 300 rifles with bayonets. Surrounded by English troops, the Continental Army was suffering severe deprivation during the winter snows while the Congress itself was enduring financial hardship. Those supplies and, above all the financial aid in "Spanish milled dollars" that Miralles distributed liberally, helped to stave off bankruptcy for the new nation.

On the other hand, Miralles detected a certain resistance among the representatives of the newly founded southern states, who feared a Spanish takeover of their territories. Miralles warned José de Gálvez about their ambivalence. On the one hand, the revolutionary leaders knew that they needed Spain's help to defeat the common enemy, but they feared the consequences of an alliance with another European empire.

Miralles' past shady dealings undoubtedly helped him negotiate with some revolutionary leaders, who hid their occasionally unspeakable interests under a banner of idealism. For example, ever present was the memory of the "Boston Tea Party," in which white colonists dressed as Indians threw bundles of tea overboard in protest of the restrictive taxes imposed by England. But it resulted in the collapse of the "Three-Cornered Trade" between Cuba and American molasses refineries and rum distilleries in Massachusetts and Rhode Island that produced hundreds of thousands of barrels of rum that afterwards were traded in African ports for slaves.

When the American Congress appointed John Adams himself to negotiate a possible peace treaty and business agreement with England in 1779, he first passed through Spain, where he was received by Diego de Gardoqui, before continuing to France. At one point, Adams declared, "I don't know why we should be embarrassed to admit that molasses was an essential ingredient in America's independence."

In this web of interests, it was almost impossible to disentangle each strand. It was evident that Juan de Miralles' priorities were not in accordance with the plans the Minister for the Indies José de Gálvez' had given to Bernardo de Gálvez. For Bernardo, the priority was to expel the English from the Mississippi Valley and the Gulf of Mexico. But for Miralles, the objective was to defeat the English in order to restore the interrupted trade between Cuba and the southern ports of the new American nation. Without question, this discrepancy in their goals meant that Don Diego Navarro and the other military leaders in Cuba did not offer their immediate support to Bernardo de Gálvez in his plan to take Pensacola. To attack the town successfully, Gálvez had asked for between 5,000 and 7,000 men, to which the captain general of Cuba responded that some 3,000 soldiers would be enough to support his campaign. When Gálvez asked commander-in-chief of the armada in Cuba, Juan Bonet, to send ships from Havana to carry out a joint military operation against Pensacola on land and by sea, the admiral flatly refused to provide the ships, which he considered indispensable for repelling a possible attack by the British fleet.

The English taking of Havana in 1762 had left deep scars among the military authorities as well as among the armada's officers who had been responsible for the port's defense. To help people understand the humiliating defeat in what had until then been thought to be the securest fortification in the Antilles, Charles III wanted to make a public example of those he considered responsible for the defeat. Because at that time the Count of Aranda occupied an important government post at the Court in Madrid, he was appointed to head the court martial adjudicating the Captain General of Cuba, the Marquis Portocarrero, considered the officer responsible for the defense of El Morro who had allowed the English into Havana when he surrendered the fort. A rigid Aranda proceeded to condemn Portocarrero and several of his aides to death. Later, a royal pardon commuted Portocarrero's sentence.

To speak in Havana of withdrawing ships and soldiers in the middle of a war with the English was like mentioning the noose in the hanged man's house.

CHAPTER 28
Mission in Pensacola

On a bleak morning in the autumn of 1780, a small schooner, that traded along the coast from the English ports of Eastern Florida to those of Western Florida, arrived from St. Augustine with Oliver Pollock on board. The ship's captain was a Scot named McIntry, who did not know what business brought Pollock to Pensacola, although he did notice the clinking of vials that could be medicine in his passenger's leather bag. Pollock had preferred not to use a disguise that was too obvious and might look suspicious; his hair piece could fly off with a gust of wind and the make-up to hide his freckles could melt away under the tropical sun's rays. He did, however, shave off his red sideburns and he dyed his copper mop of hair black. Because his Irish brogue was so pronounced, Pollock gave up trying to change his pronunciation, although he did attempt to disguise any other trace that would give him away.

Pollock did not dare forge General Clinton's letter of response, as Gálvez had proposed. Clinton's writing style could have been different from his own, or perhaps his letterhead could have changed for some reason. Attempting to emerge unscathed from such a delicate mission, Pollock decided that the best strategy was possibly the simplest: he would present himself to the commander of Fort Pensacola and verbally indicate to Campbell that General Clinton had dared not send him instructions in writing because of the danger of American corsairs or a Spanish war ship intercepting the letter. That is to say, he was giving the lie the veneer of truth.

To ride out the southwest headwinds on arriving at the latitude of Santa Rosa Island, Captain McIntry had to give a wide berth to the entrance to Pensacola Bay and then tack, hugging the wind to enter the very narrow channel between the western point of the island and the cliffs off its portside, called the Barrancas Coloradas by the Spaniards and the Red Cliffs by the English.

Even before the English built their battery there, that steep stronghold had a menacing look: its sides eaten away by erosion and seagull nests, deep cracks in the rock that looked like wrinkles on a monstrous face. It reminded Oliver of a woodcut print of the coast by his parents' home in the small town of Mermaid; old-timers said those cliffs were a giant's head petrified by a witch's spell. It was the first time he had seen the Pensacola cliffs close up; the afternoon light flooded the reddish grooves of cracks as if they were open wounds. He knew that the Redcoat garrison controlling the entrance to the bay could inflict greater wounds with their cannons.

When the schooner entered the narrow channel, whose depth varied with the shifting of sand banks, Pollock noticed the ship's prow was heading directly towards the cliffs. The ship would be at the mercy of the Redcoat cannons. Pollock removed his watch from his waistcoat and carefully noted in his notebook the time it took (four and a half minutes) for the schooner to cross the stretch of the channel below the bluff of the Red Cliffs. Any ship passing through there would need the same amount of time and be exposed to cannon fire from above. He also took note of the approximate distance between the center of the channel and the far western end of Santa Rosa Island, where the English had placed another battery that would subject any enemy ship daring to pass through there to heavy crossfire. When the ship's captain asked him what he was drawing, Pollock replied he was a landscape artist.

Once the schooner crossed the bay's tranquil waters and entered the port, Pollock returned his notebook to his pocket and swallowed hard, going over mentally what he intended to say to General Campbell, that is, if he even had a chance to speak to him. But things that seem difficult at first glance are sometimes the easiest. A pair of English grenadiers did not ask him too many questions or ask him for more identification than an old safe-conduct pass he had used in the British colonies; the pass bore the name of one Robert Maguire. The grenadiers then accompanied him to the general's office at Fort George.

When Pollock said he was bringing General Clinton's verbal instructions, and that only he could give them to General Campbell, Aide-de-camp John Moore, who was also Irish, recognized his countryman's accent immediately. Perhaps because of this simple affinity with Moore, the visitor did not have to wait even five minutes. When Pollock entered the commandant's office, General Campbell received him with a familiarity Pollock thought exaggerated. The general was wearing a red uniform, whose buttons and each metal belt buckle were scrupulously polished. The general's rosy cheeks seemed to indicate a fondness for spirits, but his elegant demeanor seemed to attest to his noble origins. Pollock recognized in Campbell the Anglo-Saxon aristocratic bearing that, with exquisite manners and a phlegmatic smile, had subjugated half of humanity, including the poor Irish people—it did not matter that the general was of Scottish origin.

"So, two Irish bandits have gathered here: you, Mr. Maguire, and my aide John Moore," said the general in jest. "I see that, not content to give me an Irish aide, General Clinton sends me a messenger of the same ilk."

"General Clinton begs your pardon for not having answered before now your letter of last May. He was too busy dealing with rebel mischief." Pollock used the expression "mischief" with which the Royalists minimized the successful maneuvers of Washington's army in the North.

"I understand very well what you're saying, Mr. Maguire. I assume that General Clinton has been informed of our necessities. Did the general let you read my letter?"

"Indeed, he wanted me to read the letter to grasp the situation it describes, which I understand is rather critical, given the possibility of a Spanish attack. As you know, the Spaniards have already taken Mobile."

"Have no doubt, Mr. Maguire, that the Spaniards will attack us and, to tell the truth, I'm surprised they haven't done so already."

"To take the town, even without the reinforcements that General Clinton decides to send you, they would need troops and ships from Havana. But, I understand, the military authorities on that island are not willing to let them have even one ship, not even one company of soldiers, for fear of repeating the English occupation that took place during the last war."

"I see you're very well informed. . . . Makes sense, as you are one of the general's closest aides. I also think the memory of our having taken Havana is possibly saving us from a Spanish attack on Pensacola, although it is also possible the Spaniards are waiting for our Indian troops to retreat from their position near the town. It's true, we are spending a fortune on feeding the savage horde, but thanks to the strenuous efforts of our Indian Department Superintendent Alexander Cameron, we've kept them as allies for the moment."

The general paused and, shrugging his shoulders, heaved a deep sigh as if it were hard for him to accept the inevitable. "Unfortunately, that pack of savages with all their war whoops and their acts of cruelty won't intimidate Mr. Gálvez, whom we know has experience fighting the Indians. That's why I've humbly insisted to General Clinton that he send reinforcements and funds to restore our fortifications, which are not in any condition to withstand an all-out attack."

His aide, who until then had not spoken, jumped in. "If I had to fight against the Spaniards, I'd prefer to do it by leaving the fort to engage them rather than remain here like a sitting duck waiting for a Spanish grenade to blow my head off."

General Campbell shook his head and scolded him, "John, you may be right, but as I've told you, do not make remarks like that in public. The troops are already demoralized just waiting for Gálvez to attack. Up until now, he's been unstoppable."

Pollock chimed in, "The young governor has earned that reputation, but we know some of his compatriots doubt whether his meteoric career is due to his own record or to the influence of his uncle, who is a very powerful cabinet minister."

By the general's expression, Pollock guessed he was surprised his visitor was up to date on the inner workings of the Spanish government. The spy then judged that the moment had arrived to hand Campbell the bottle of vintage brandy that the Spanish governor had sent as if it were from General Clinton himself.

When Campbell removed the bottle of brandy from its velvet case, he almost wept with emotion. "Dear Mr. Maguire, to gain my confidence you don't need better credentials than this bottle. It's the best proof that the commander-in-chief knows very well what my taste is . . . or rather, what my weaknesses are."

Campbell spent a few minutes in complete silence looking at the bottle and its wrapper, as if someone had just handed him the Holy Grail. Once he had put it away carefully in one of his mahogany desk drawers, he regained his military composure.

"Mr. Maguire, I would like nothing better than to uncork this bottle immediately and invite you to spend the rest of the afternoon chatting with me, however, you and I have a lot of work ahead of us. By God, it's an urgent task if we want the reinforcements to arrive in time. Although I assume you've tired after the crossing, I think the only way you yourself will realize our needs is to visit our installations and see how little we have and how much we are lacking."

If Pollock himself had asked the general to show him the fortifications, his request would have sounded suspicious. Being that the offer came from the general himself, Pollock only had to give thanks to St. Patrick that his mission was turning out splendidly. When imagining the dangers he would face on this mission, which had led him to write his last will and testament, he never dreamed he'd be received so well by the general himself.

Now that the wind seemed to be blowing in his favor, he took advantage to ask Campbell, "Would you mind, Your Excellency, if I jot down a few observations in my notebook? I'd like to be able to write up the best possible report for the commander-in-chief."

The general himself, along with his aide Moore and two grenadiers accompanied Pollock on a tour of the fortifications. They led the way down a path covered in sand and past some long-faced

Indians to the forts protecting Pensacola, which were laid out in a semi-circle on the top of sandy Gage Hill.

"Please don't repeat this to General Clinton," said Campbell on seeing how his shiny, leather riding boots were sinking into the sand, "but do you really believe it's worth sacrificing lives and supplies to defend this sand pit in the middle of nowhere?"

Moore threw a reproachful glance at the general, who had just warned his aide not to demoralize the troops.

Of the forts built on Gage Hill, the most resilient was Fort George, situated about one thousand two hundred yards from the Pensacola city center; it housed the general's headquarters and was the only one that had been reinforced recently, now protected by a double stockade with a moat full of sand between the walls.

Three hundred yards from Ft. George, there was a small fort defending the principal fort, called the Prince of Wales, which had an elliptical shape. Another was called the Queen's Fort, located at the same distance from Ft. George. The general pointed out to his guest the numerous weaknesses in the defenses along the line of the hill: walls fallen, dismantled wooden barriers, cannons still not set in their positions, all because of lack of construction materials. There were some rusted cannons that Campbell himself declared useless.

The spy was taking detailed notes on each one of the defense's weaknesses, believing that, if he succeeded in returning to New Orleans, his report would sound like music to Gálvez's ears. It was hard for Pollock not to smile every time Campbell himself asked him to note some flaw the visitor seemed not to have noticed.

CHAPTER 29
The Ducks in the Bay

After finishing the inspection of the Gage Hill forts, General Campbell next turned to the Red Cliffs fort, a true jewel among the otherwise mediocre fortifications; that way, Pollock's report to General Clinton would not be completely negative. They climbed into a small two-wheeled trap carriage, drawn by a pair of mules, that could barely negotiate the hill's steep slope, which was slippery from the sand the sea breeze blew across that stretch of road.

Upon arriving at the promontory's point, Pollock took in the imposing scene from Fort Red Cliffs. Sadly, he realized, the fort's batteries completely dominated the channel waters below. General Campbell proceeded to show his guest the magnificent construction of the installations protecting the battery, made up of five thirty-two-inch cannons and another six six-inch cannons that were pointing towards the promontory's flanks. As if he were a child showing a friend a valuable toy, the general showed Pollock each one of the cannons, which he himself had dubbed with a name that had been engraved in copper on each weapon meaning to inspire fear in the enemy.

"Observe, Maguire, my friend. Those cannons completely dominate the only access channel to the bay," Campbell said as he handed his spyglass to his guest. "If you observe how the channel bends at the very foot of the promontory, you'll understand that any ship having to change direction from the open sea to enter the mouth of that narrow passage must necessarily line up its prow exactly with our batteries . . . and the ship will be at our mercy from the front, the side and then the rear."

Campbell gave one of the cannons an affectionate pat, like the caress a rider gives his favorite mount, and added, "So, it's practically impossible for those ships not to be damaged."

Seeing the confidence the general had in that battery, Pollock ventured to ask, "Excellency, for me to give General Clinton a complete report about my visit, would it be too much to ask for the artillerymen to set off a few shots to show me?" The Irishman was sure that Campbell's pride would oblige him.

"Of course, we would be delighted to give a demonstration! I would have suggested it myself, but as we are a bit short on gunpowder and munitions, I wouldn't want General Clinton to think we're wasting them on demonstrations."

The general then pointed out to the artilleryman a target about twelve hundred feet away, in the middle of the channel, the place where the waters were darkest over which at that moment a great flock of aquatic birds was diving.

"Go ahead, Sergeant. I beg you to blow to smithereens those silly birds daring to challenge His Majesty's batteries." He then turned to Pollock and asked him to step back a bit from the cannon. "Those thirty-two-inch cannons are so powerful that it's not a good idea to be too close when they fire. I also suggest you cover your ears."

Campbell himself gave the order to fire, and the cannon spit its deadly load with a deafening explosion, which made its gun carriage recoil several yards. The cloud of smoke took a few seconds to dissipate, but when Pollock observed with the spyglass the place where the cannonball had fallen, he knew the projectile had not hit the target. The volley had struck six hundred feet farther than the blue patch, in clearer waters with a sandy bottom.

Stunned, the general was speechless for a moment, but then tried to minimize the miss. "Come on, Sergeant Douglas, don't be so shy with a flock of ducks. If you succeed in hitting them, I'll send a long boat to recover the game, and the chef can prepare Duck à l'Orange, even if it is a French dish. I beg you take more accurate aim to show our illustrious guest how we at the Red Cliffs shoot."

Again and again, with the booms and puffs of smoke that momentarily engulfed the firing platform, the gunners shot off several different cannons without hitting any of the ducks in the flock that had landed smoothly in the middle of the channel. As they kept missing the target, Campbell's mood became progressively bad; at first, he mocked the men and then resorted to dressing down the lieutenant commanding the battery.

"Mr. Long, it's evident that your men haven't practiced much in the past few months. I hope that what you've saved in gunpowder and munitions you haven't spent on liquor. What is certain is that in a few days I'll be coming back through here. We'll put a leaking launch in the channel, and we'll put the artillery man who can't sink it to work on the moat at the Queen's Fort."

The lieutenant became so red-faced at seeing himself reprimanded in front of all his men that he was speechless. Campbell and his colleagues were on their way back to the fort, when there was an incident that could have cost the Irishman his life, if he hadn't kept a cool head. They were nearing the carriage, when the visitor heard someone shouting behind him, "Pollock! Oliver Pollock!"

Pollock ignored the man calling to him and continued chatting with the general's aide without ever turning his head. However, he had no choice but to stop when someone touched his shoulder. One of the battery guards had thought he recognized him as an old childhood friend, but when Pollock turned, the man could see he had very dark hair.

"Pardon me, Sir. I thought I recognized someone I knew years ago. You're not Oliver Pollock, are you?"

"My friend," answered the spy with aplomb, "I assure you, I've never heard that name in my life."

Given the forcefulness of his answer, the perplexed grenadier just stared at him and dared to add timidly, "It's odd, because the person I'm talking about is also Irish and your accent seems Irish. But it's a good thing you aren't Pollock, because someone told me he had gone over to the rebel side and oversees getting arms and supplies to the crooks up North."

Then the general's aide, who probably had felt insulted since he too was an Irishman, blurted out, "Leave us alone, my good man, and try not to see things that aren't there. Or perhaps you think all Irishmen are traitors to the King?"

Pollock exhaled with relief, knowing the aide's pride had probably saved his life that day. General Campbell, who was walking far ahead of them with great strides that showed his indignation, never even found out about the incident. In fact, the general was so displeased, he said not a word during the trip back to the fort.

Only when they alighted from the trap carriage did Campbell comment in a low voice to his guest, so no one else could hear him, "Mr. Maguire, let me assure you that this failure won't be repeated in the future. For the sake of our budding friendship, I would ask you kindly not to include in your report to his Excellency General Clinton any reference to what you have seen today at Red Cliffs. It was an accident that won't happen again. Now, I invite you to come up to my rooms to taste that brandy you so kindly brought on behalf of his Excellency."

The sun was setting on the waters of the bay when Pollock took one last look at the Red Cliffs from the fort's battlements and noticed the flock of mallards still darting to and fro at the bottom of the cliffs.

CHAPTER 30
An *in articulo mortis* Wedding
(Bernardo de Gálvez speaks)

On my return from the Mobile expedition, I continued lodging at the Capuchin monastery, trying to avoid adding fuel to the fire of gossip that was already spreading around the city about my romance with Felicitas. I continued to visit the St. Maxent home frequently, where, after every evening's dinner, the rest of the family would kindly leave me alone with Felicitas on the veranda that looked out on the great river. At dusk a voluptuous breeze, heavy with exotic aromas, would emanate from the reeds growing along the shore.

One night, I noticed Felicitas was nervously stammering and wringing the lacy hankie she always carried in her hands. No sooner had I asked her if she was worried about something, she began to sob, covering her face with her hankie. I was greatly alarmed and, I confess, the first thing I thought was that I could have gotten her with child in one of our romantic encounters in the moonlight.

"Felicitas, tell me what's wrong. If your displeasure has something to do with me, I beg you, please feel free to tell me. If I've hurt you in any way, please let me make amends."

She calmed down on hearing my words and, wiping the tears from her beautiful face, she spoke in a halting voice. "If what I've been told is true, it will be hard for you to atone for a sin that probably happened some years ago."

I became somewhat indignant and, above all, surprised that anyone had borne false witness against me.

"I can assure you on my honor that I have never ever committed a shameful sin. I almost prefer not to know who has been so vile as to turn you against me because, I'll lay his head at his feet . . . " Just as I said it, I remembered this was the expression my uncle José had used when, in a bout of madness, he had wanted to cow an officer who had disagreed with his decision-making. I immediately regretted having spoken that very same phrase. "Dear Felicitas, you don't have to tell me who slandered me, but if you would at least tell me what I'm accused of, I'm sure I'll be able to answer any accusation to your satisfaction."

Felicitas relaxed considerably and explained to me what had caused her to worry so. Apparently, a little before I had arrived in New Orleans, a witch or diviner whom she sometimes consulted had seen a man, who by all accounts was myself, in a vision. In the good part of her vision she had predicted that Cupid would bring Felicitas and me together. In the bad part, the woman was convinced that at some point in the past I had committed a nefarious crime that I would have to expiate. The witch had warned Felicitas that, if I did not redeem myself for that sin, the Father of Waters would unleash all his power against me.

Faced with such a ridiculous accusation, based on a slave's vision, I could not think of anything to say. Instead of guessing what I might have done, I took her in my arms and kissed her passionately as I never had done before, thinking for a moment I was going to lose her.

Felicitas embraced me too, surrendering to me. When I broke our embrace, I noticed my arms and legs, my whole body was shaking as if I were poisoned with quicksilver. Indeed, I was an *azogado* because she had poisoned me with love.

The next day, I again returned to Gilbert Antoine de St. Maxent's home, this time to ask for his daughter's hand in marriage, to which the gentleman agreed. However, it also seemed to me I should warn him that as the governor of Louisiana, I would ask the King's permission to marry, as my predecessor Luis de Unzuaga had done to be able to marry St. Maxent's other daughter, Isabel. It would be a huge obstacle to marry before leaving for the campaign against the

English. I informed my future father-in-law what the Capuchin prior had said to me about the wedding *in articulo mortis*. St. Maxent did not think it a bad idea and even helped me to make up a fake illness to facilitate this kind of wedding.

I would leave the city for a few days and would return apparently gravely ill, after taking a potion from the same witch who had spoken to Felicitas about a supposed sin in my past. Since I had already planned a trip up river to verify the state of the English forts we had attacked weeks ago, I used the ruse of complaining to my aides that I was not feeling well during the trip. Once I ingested the witch's emetic, I did indeed feel unwell. I began to vomit and had chills as if I really had succumbed to ague.

I felt a bit ashamed when I found out the news had spread through the whole city that the governor had fallen seriously ill on his trip. Some churches were even conducting religious services for my recovery. So that I could be cared for during my supposed affliction, I returned to the Capuchin monastery, whose prior had been responsible up to a point for this intrigue. Father René Lambert had prepared everything, including having arranged for a double bed in his cell and having the bed made up with fine-quality sheets and two large pillows. The afternoon of the wedding ceremony, I got undressed and put on a long silk nightshirt that, depending on the circumstances, could be used for a shroud or for a dress shirt. For greater realism, the monk applied some dark make-up under my eyes that made me look moribund.

When Felicitas' younger sisters entered the cell and saw me in that state, they burst into tears. Obviously they were not in on the secret. The bride's father, who also served as my best man, entered with the bride on her arm. She wore a plain, dark dress that flattered her graceful curves. Her hair was covered with a black mantilla and draped on her shoulders was a Manila shawl embroidered with flowers and butterflies. Her wardrobe would have been appropriate either at a formal wedding or a funeral.

When everything was ready, a Gregorian chant was heard coming from the monastery corridor and a procession of Capuchin monks, preceded by an altar boy swinging a censer, entered the cell.

The prior did not officiate the wedding ceremony. Instead, it was Friar Cirilo de Barcelona, the General Curate of Louisiana, whom Brother Lambert had enlisted in the intrigue, despite the French Capuchins and the Spanish curate's monastic order not getting along well. After positioning himself at the head of the bed, where I was propped up, the Vicar pronounced the Latin liturgical words for a wedding in *articulo mortis*, which sounded to me too much like what I had heard at funerals.

The scene was so perfect that I took on the role of the dying man and almost wept, thinking that this young and beautiful woman, who had been already been married once, could very soon be widowed a second time. When Felicitas touched her hand to my chest while we were exchanging rings, my half-opened eyes contemplated the woman who was to be my wife. She was so modest and yet so sensuous that I realized I was becoming aroused, unexpectedly lifting the sheets that were covering me to the point that it almost made the cruets containing the holy oils fall over on the bed. Fortunately, I managed to control that carnal impulse immediately, thinking that I would be committing a great sin by pitching a tent while I was being given extreme unction.

As soon as I was left alone with the woman who was now my wife I was again overcome by uncontrollable desire, perhaps because that half-funeral, half-celebration proved a powerful aphrodisiac. Felicitas must have sensed what I was feeling because she quietly shut the cell door and tumbled into bed next to me. With the greatest finesse, I undressed her little by little, undoing her petticoat laces and revealing her satiny skin, which by the light of the large candles the monks had left there, was turning out to be a delicacy I fervently wanted to caress, lick and bite.

That night, the walls of the cell that had been built as a house of prayer and penitence were shaken by uncommon tremors.

Part Four

CHAPTER 31
Prayers to the Father of Waters

"If the sea does not smite us again, I hope that, God willing, we'll be happy because everything that is happening is under my orders, including the sailors."

On February 17, 1781, Bernardo de Gálvez departed from the port of Havana at the head of a military convoy headed for English Pensacola. He recorded in his diary the immense satisfaction he felt on having been able to assemble several ships and enough troops to undertake the town's conquest. After several failed expeditions, the last doomed by a terrifying hurricane, it would seem the Gulf waters wanted to punish the pride and ambition of the Louisiana governor once again.

The first thrashing Gálvez referred to had been suffered by the small flotilla of vessels that had treveled up the Mississippi's left bank to take the English forts, when a tremendous downpour decimated it. The second thrashing was suffered by another Gálvez fleet that had left New Orleans for Mobile, when a storm made the ships run aground on treacherous shoals at the river's mouth and later smashed these ships against the coast.

Nature's third and severest blow to Gálvez's plans occurred after Gálvez had convinced the reticent members of the War Council in Havana to let him lead a squadron of twenty-eight war ships and a transport convoy with more than three thousand men for a joint operation in Pensacola Bay. He had barely passed the Florida peninsula and sailed into the Gulf when a huge gale battered the squadron and the convoy for more than eighty hours. The hurricane winds knocked down the masts of twenty-three ships, scattering the squadron throughout the Gulf. Some ships ended up in New Orleans, others in Mobile, and several ships sought refuge from the storm in San Bernardo Bay on the Texas coast. There, one of the ships was attacked by the coastal Indians, who killed the entire crew and set fire to the ship.

Despite these adverse conditions, Gálvez had the pluck to stay on board the convoy's flag ship, the frigate Nuestra Señora de la O, riding out the storm and trying to gather the ships that had survived the disaster to continue the Pensacola expedition. However, the sad state of the men and the ships made it impossible to lay a difficult and prolonged siege to the strongest English fort on the Gulf of Mexico.

Gálvez had barely returned to Havana when, with his usual tenacity, he called the War Council together again to propose a new expedition with the same mission, which was to cost even more than the last one. Although His Majesty the King had appointed him commander-in-chief of naval and ground forces for the taking of Pensacola, Gálvez only encountered skepticism and a lack of enthusiasm among the military and naval authorities. Especially since the naval authorities blamed the squadron's latest disaster on Gálvez, who had not listened to their advice when they had predicted the storm.

In the interest of expediting the Pensacola campaign, Charles III had appointed a royal commissioner for the campaign, Francisco de Saavedra, a close friend of Gálvez since the military academy. The commissioner's vessel had been boarded by an English war ship, and he had been held in Jamaica for a few months. After being freed, Saavedra arrived in Havana and contributed to easing the tensions in the War Council, finally convincing the naval authorities to give Gálvez another squadron, albeit a much smaller one. The news that the English had launched an attack on Mobile also contributed to overcoming the War Council's opposition. They finally decided that the war ships and the transport convoy should aid the Spaniards besieged at Mobile first and that, only after taking Mobile, would they attempt to lay siege to Pensacola.

Gálvez was not very devout, but on the eve of his departure he went to the chapel at the El Morro fort, whose chaplain, Gil de Santiváñez, he knew well.

When the chaplain saw Gálvez enter the church, he nodded in greeting and said, "The Holy Scriptures say God smiles when a sinner repents and returns to the fold, more than he does for a hundred good men who have their place in Paradise already assured," joked Santivañez. "In addition to being happy to see you within these holy walls, I confess I am dying of curiosity to know what brings Your Excellency to visit your humble servant. I assume you must have your hands full with making the final preparations for the convoy's departure."

"Although some people think I'm a non-believer, I've come by the church in part because without divine intervention, I never would have been able to gather such a powerful force. I also want to give you this purse to beg you to say several Masses and Novenas to help us achieve very specific goals: pray for the squadron's successful voyage and for the Father of Waters' blessing for this operation."

The priest stared at Gálvez, perplexed. Then, he placed his hands under his robe's sackcloth bib and said, "Your Excellency has always managed to surprise me with unusual witticisms. But what you're asking truly astounds me. How can I pray to the Father of Waters, when his patronage does not appear on any list of saints or any litany I'm familiar with?"

"Well, it's about time you priests and monks understand that in these latitudes, some powers prevail that aren't on our list of saints," Gálvez shot back. "Besides, is there reason to believe that the God who quelled the storm over Lake Tiberias and who in ancient times saved Jonah from the belly of the whale wouldn't want to get along with those who rule the winds and tides? You do want to help me to be successful in this enterprise that the King himself has entrusted to me and that three times running has been foiled by the forces of nature, do you not?"

Since the priest had frequently been at sea and knew the fury of rough waters, he did not want to provoke Gálvez's anger, so he put Gálvez's purse in his pocket and acquiesced. "Amen, let us pray for the Father of Waters and for God to protect you during the crossing."

CHAPTER 32
The Red Cliffs

When Commander-in-Chief Gálvez woke up in the early morning, he heard all the Havana church bells ringing farewell to the squadron and the convoy. After carefully buttoning his jacket, he strapped on his sword and went up to the flag ship's quarterdeck to watch the fleet sail away. Once the heavy chain that was blocking access to the dock had been lifted, a parade commenced of seven war ships, six frigates, several polacres, long boats, sloops, vessels and brigantines, not to mention a schooner loaded exclusively with salt and liquor for the Indians who were serving as aides to the expedition.

As commander of the whole operation, Gálvez was sailing aboard the flag ship San Ramón. In its hold there were a hundred and fifty thousand *pesos* for campaign expenses, in addition to the necessary supplies. When the San Ramón unfurled its imposing sails and the ship's graceful silhouette passed below the fort's chapel, Gálvez could not help smiling as he recalled the face the priest had made when he was asked to include the Father of Waters in his prayers.

In the officers' cabin, José Calvo de Irazábal, the ship's captain and commander of the expedition's naval forces, was meeting with other captains. When Gálvez came down from the quarterdeck to join them, none of the sailors bothered to stand up to greet him. He thought, perhaps, he had been premature in noting in his diary how satisfied he was with the whole expedition, including the sailors under his command. A few days before the convoy's departure, Captain Calvo de Irazábal had addressed a note to Admiral Juan Bautista Bonet to ask if during the Pensacola expedition, he should act as a subordinate and obey Gálvez's orders. The head of the fleet had answered, "You must do so and obey Don Bernardo's orders relating to the conquest of Pensacola, but you should put them into practice using your own intellect without deviating from the Armada's Royal Ordinances." This response was so ambiguous that under certain circumstances it could be interpreted as an excuse to disobey Gálvez's orders, when those orders contradicted naval ordinances. To avoid provoking new tensions, Gálvez had tolerated an outburst or two, thinking that it was not worth quibbling with the Armada over protocol. But he would soon realize that Captain Calvo de Irazábal's and his officers' disregard extended beyond matters of protocol, given that these captains believed Gálvez should not deviate from the instructions given to Gálvez for the Pensacola campaign by his War Council superiors, including Admiral Juan Bonet.

When the squadron was nearing the Florida coast, a packet boat arrived from Mobile with news that the city's defenders had valiantly repulsed the English attack. Because he no longer needed to go to Mobile, Gálvez decided to send the squadron directly to Pensacola, but that would mean deviating from the initial plan approved by the War Council in Havana. Captain Calvo then invited the land and naval commanders to meet on the San Ramón to assess the situation. Wanting to please all of the forces under his command, Bernardo de Gálvez did not object to this request and explained at length to the gathered officers the siege he had been planning. Although unenthusiastic, Captain Calvo and his officers accepted the new strategy on the condition they would be able to weigh in when the squadron arrived at the objective.

During the crossing, Bernardo de Gálvez used the time remaining before arriving in Pensacola Bay to show the naval officers area maps and the location of the various forts protecting the city. Since Pensacola was protected by three forts fanned out on a hill, Gálvez thought it was essential that the siege be carried out simultaneously by land and by sea. To that end, the Spanish ships should cross the channel connecting the open sea with the bay. The problem that especially worried the naval officers was that to enter the bay from the open sea, the ships had to sail through a very narrow channel.

There, they would be under cross fire from two batteries: on the port side, from the Red Cliffs, and on the starboard side from the fort located on the far western side of Santa Rosa Island, called Punta Sigüenza. It occurred to Gálvez that to avert this danger, even in part, would require landing ground troops on Santa Rosa Island before the fleet tried to enter the port. If they landed according to plan, the troops of grenadiers and infantry would attack from the rear of the small fort at Punta Sigüenza, which was much more accessible than the Red Cliffs batteries. Once this fort was neutralized, at least the Spanish ships would not be subjected to the cross fire of both batteries.

In the meeting held on board the San Ramón a little before arriving off the coast of Pensacola, Gálvez so clearly explained the combined attack strategy of the army and the armada that many of the officers supported it. They included some of the ship captains who expressed a desire for their ships to be the first to enter the channel, once the ground troops had silenced the Punta Sigüenza cannons.

A little before arriving at Pensacola, the fleet incorporated several ships that had left Havana a little after the rest of the fleet, among them the brigantine Galvezton. Some American corsairs had captured it from the English on the Mississippi and made it a gift to Governor Gálvez. In contrast to the Armada's other war ships, this small brigantine and its captain, Pedro Rousseau, fell under Bernardo de Gálvez's direct command. It was a double-masted ship with a tapered bowsprit built to take advantage of even the slightest breeze in its quadrangular sails, its stays, its jibs and its great triangular sail, which served as its main sail. The governor decided to move on board the Galvezton with the pretext that it was more maneuverable than the flag ship. From there he would be able to direct the landing maneuver more easily; the truth was that during the entire crossing he had felt uncomfortable on board the San Ramón, whose captain had at no time relaxed his haughty and disrespectful attitude.

In the early morning hours, the pilots recognized the outline of Santa Rosa Island, which had the shape of an uncommonly large whale beached on the sand as if it were protecting the interior waters of Pensacola Bay. Although the sea was not completely calm, the landing took place without incident. As soon as they reached land,

Colonel Francisco Longoria's troops headed to Point Sigüenza in complete silence and in total darkness to take the English battery located there. At the first light of day, however, they saw that the bastion had been abandoned, and only three unmounted cannons and a battery of half-fallen down walls remained.

When he heard the news, Gálvez went back on board the San Ramón and proposed that Captain Calvo enter the port according to the plan agreed upon at the last meeting, although they had not verified the channel's shape and depth. Gálvez proposed the frigates and other lighter craft attempt going in first, leaving for last the entrance of the San Ramón, the largest ship in the squadron. But Captain Calvo insisted that, as commander of the flag ship, he should be the first to face enemy fire. An argument broke out when Gálvez asked Calvo to allow him to remain on board while they sailed through the channel, but the captain absolutely refused to give him the privilege. To avoid an incident at such a crucial moment, Gálvez yielded to the captain and returned to the Galvezton. From the brigantine, he did observe, however, that, after approaching the coast, while it was still far from the reach of the English canons, the San Ramón heaved to after an odd maneuver and again anchored even though all the other war ships were waiting to follow it.

Another argument ensued when Gálvez returned to the San Ramón and found that Calvo was beside himself. In almost insulting terms, Calvo insisted that because he had tried to carry out Gálvez's instructions, the ship had hit a sand bar and, after losing a few bottom planks, he had had to lighten the load to free the ship, blowing the ballast and throwing overboard water, firewood and even cattle fodder. Gálvez responded that the mishap would not have occurred if they had heeded him by placing the frigates at the head of the convoy. In the heated exchange, Calvo again insisted that the problem was their departure from the initial plan approved by the War Council in Havana.

During this time, the weather had changed and Gálvez began to fear that the gale winds that were very frequent along those coasts could blow at any moment, forcing the squadron and the convoy to weigh anchor. That would have stranded the army on land. At

Calvo's request, Gálvez agreed to meet to consult again on board the San Ramón. Now, the same captains who a few hours earlier had quarreled over the honor of being the first to face enemy fire refused to venture their ships into the channel after their leader's ship had sustained minor damage. First, Gálvez made clear to them that if the warships did not enter the port, a change in the weather could make the whole operation fail. Captain Calvo advocated defending the fleet under his command at all costs. He argued that the channel was so narrow that if enemy fire succeeded in knocking down the masts or sinking the first war ship, the sunken ship would block the next ship's passage. If that happened, he asserted, then some ships would collide with others before they could turn to avoid the crash.

CHAPTER 33
I Alone

The captains were still arguing when a sloop arrived under the command of Lt. Juan de Riaño with the news that Colonel José de Ezpeleta had arrived with nine hundred men near the Los Perdidos River, located only five leagues from Pensacola. Although it was good news, it added to Gálvez's mounting concern that, if his fleet abandoned them, even more troops would be exposed on land, helpless.

Taking the plunge, on the afternoon of March 14, 1781, Gálvez ordered the Galvezton captain to plumb the depth of the channel to find out how many fathoms there were to the bottom at the channel mouth. Once he knew that, Gálvez decided that with a small flotilla consisting of the Galvezton, Juan de Riaño's sloop and two gunboats directly under his command, he had sufficient naval personnel and equipment to enter the port. Once he had made this decision, Gálvez sent Engineering Officer Francisco de Paula Gelabert to the San Ramón to speak to Captain Calvo and the other captains. Sailors and cabin boys alike stopped scurrying among the rigging to witness the messenger's approach, wondering what the message was, because they all knew that the relationship between the two men had practically been severed.

Once on the quarterdeck, Gelabert opened a leather bag, and a round object rolled out and fell heavily at Captain Calvo's feet as he read the message aloud: "I am conveying and present to you, one cannonball of 32-inch, the same used by the Red Cliffs battery. Let the brave and honorable follow me. The Galvezton will lead the fleet to banish your fear."

Captain Calvo de Irazábal was for a moment paralyzed at the magnitude of the insult, but then stood tall with his hand gripping his sword's hilt and shouted, "The general is a reckless, spoiled brat, a traitor to King and country. I shall lay before the King's feet his personal insult to me and the insult to the entire navy. He is the coward who skulked behind his own cannons, not I." Glaring at Officer Gelabert, he added, "And, such a message from Gálvez should have been brought by a lowly sailor and not by an officer, so I might have the satisfaction of hanging him from the yardarm!"

Gelabert said nothing, picked up the cannonball rolling around the deck with the ship's rocking and withdrew.

At 2:30 p.m., Gálvez boarded the Galvezton, which was waiting for him anchored at the very mouth of the channel leading to the bay. The first person he saw on deck was Oliver Pollock, who pressed him for permission to accompany him.

"Under no circumstances. I'm the leader of this expedition and I should go alone! Alone!" Gálvez said in a tone that admitted no rebuttal. A moment late, he added with a smile, "I hope the information about the Red Cliffs you gave me is right, but if not, I doubt I'll have the chance to ask you to explain yourself."

"Remember, Excellency, you should stay as close as possible to Punta de Sigüenza, because the battery cannons cannot reach the other side of the channel. May St. Patrick protect you!"

Forthwith, Gálvez commanded Captain Rousseau to raise the flag with the image of a bugle on the foresail, the icon of supreme commander of the expedition, and to fire the cannons on board for the statutory salvo to let the Red Cliffs gunners know who was on board that small craft."

When the Galvezton unfurled its sail, the sloop captained by Juan de Riaño and two gunboats followed him at a certain distance. The southeasterly winds died down, but a late afternoon breeze made the flotilla's sails billow on course for the cliffs where the English batteries were located. The scene of four small boats sailing slowly by the foot of the monumental promontory could have appeared idyllic to anyone who did not know what was in play.

The Red Cliffs' gunners, who heard the cannon fire and observed the bugle on the foresail indicating the military rank of the man sailing on the brigantine, knew they would never again have a more desirable target in their sights. They murmured prayers and oaths for their cannonballs to sink the Galvezton. Suddenly, the roar of five 32-inch cannons firing simultaneously split the silence of the bay. Moments later, other explosions of smaller caliber fire shook the stone fort.

From the deck of the Spanish ships waiting outside the channel and from the beach of Santa Rosa Island, where the already disembarked troops were gathered, the sailors and dragoons held their breath, afraid to hear a mast splitting from a grenade exploding or to see the brigantine sinking in the channel. Every time a cannon missed the target and fell into the water, creating a splash, the Santa Rosa Island grenadiers who had been following the flotilla's trajectory burst into shouts and applause as they ran along the beach.

For four and a half minutes, smoke from the discharges floated over the channel and hid the sight of the flotilla from the Spanish troops. But afterward, a breeze dissipated the smoke, and Gálvez's flotilla could be seen reaching the bay's waters, where the cannonballs could not hit the ships. At that moment, the echo of a thunderous ovation crossed the channel and was heard at the top of the Red Cliffs: "Long live the King of Spain! Long live Gálvez!"

Captain Calvo, who had followed the Galvezton's progress with his spyglass and observed Gálvez seated under the wheelhouse during the whole crossing, felt terribly humiliated and retreated to his cabin to avoid hearing his crew's applause. Within minutes, the other captains stood before him to ask permission to follow the example the Galvezton had set for them. Calvo at first denied his authorization and even went so far as to give instructions for all ships to maintain their position, not even to repair their moorings, but his officers' insistence was so strong that Calvo de Irazábal was forced to allow the Spanish ships to enter the bay.

The next day, the frigates and the rest of the convoy followed the same path as the Galvezton, without suffering any mishaps worth mentioning, despite the one hundred and forty cannonballs shot from the Red Cliffs. Calvo, however, was no longer on site to see the war ships' achievement, because that same day the San Ramón had weighed anchor in the wee hours of the morning and sailed for Havana.

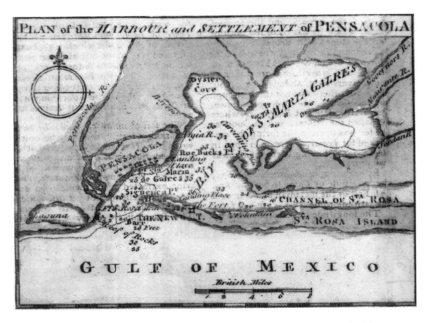

By J. Gibson—From Maps ETC at the University of South Florida

CHAPTER 34
The Bear Skin
(Bernardo de Gálvez speaks)

Although my family had never seen a bear in the Málaga mountains, where we're from, I remember that my grandfather used to say nobody should try to sell a bear's skin before killing the bear. My grandfather was always right.

After the huge effort I had made to gather the expeditionary forces for the siege of Pensacola, after quelling the resistance of the army and naval authorities in Havana and after having risked my neck by the bay's entrance, I finally found myself in the vicinity of the town where the reinforcement troops that had been sent from New Orleans and Mobile were camped. I thought the rest of the campaign would be a walk in the park. But I soon realized that the most important part of the battle was yet to begin. My grandfather's proverbial bear kept most of his claws and fangs and was willing to sell his tough hide at a high price.

Our dragoons had barely disembarked on the beach on the other side of the bay, when we received a hail of cannonballs from the English artillerymen, who sewed death and confusion among our ranks. We had not expected such a reaction from the enemy. Without giving us time to get into our launches again, a swarm of Indians, who had been hiding in the trees that grew at the top of the mound, ran down the hill howling hair-raising whoops and attacked the wounded lying on the beach with their hatchets and knives. The Indians withdrew as quickly as they had arrived, leaving a bloody trail of dead soldiers on the sand dunes.

When I asked Captain St. Maxent, Gilbert Antoine's son, where the Indians had come from, he confirmed they belonged to the Choctaw, Creek and Seminole tribes, who could be terribly cruel, just as the chronicles of the first Spanish explorers in Florida had described. St. Maxent reminded me that the English traders had been selling liquor and arms to them for a long time, and it probably did not take much for the British military authorities to convince them to help fight the American colonists. Those same colonists had invaded Cherokee territory, shed their blood some time ago and expelled them from their ancestral lands. At war, it was all the same to the Indians whether they killed a rebel colonist or a Spanish soldier.

Another obstacle I would encounter during the siege of Pensacola was the less than gentlemanly behavior of John Campbell, the commander of the British forces. Oliver Pollock had described General Campbell as a consummate and pleasant gentleman on the surface, but one capable of pettiness. One of the Indian auxiliary troops that arrived in Santa Rosa with Ezpeleta warned me of Campbell's lack of respect for the rules of war. The Indian had heard it from a deserter from his own tribe, who said the general had given orders to burn or destroy anything that could serve as parapet in order to avoid the Spanish army's attacking English positions by using houses in the city.

On March 20, 1781, I sent a message to Campbell stating,

Your Excellency. Dear Sir:

At the risk of being treated with the utmost severity, the English in Havana threatened us not to destroy, burn or disable the King's as well as private factories and war ships. I warn you in kind, your Excellency and any others to whom these conditions may apply.

Field Headquarters on Santa Rosa Island
March 20, 1781
Your faithful servant, Bernardo de Gálvez

General Campbell sent an arrogant and belligerent response, unworthy of a soldier and even less of a gentleman:

Dear Sir,

We dismiss any enemy threat against us as a ploy or strategy of war. . . . I shall not do anything contrary to the rules and customs of war in my defense of Pensacola (inasmuch as I am the one being attacked). I consider myself in your debt, given that Your Excellency holds me in such high esteem. I assure you that my conduct concerning the city of Pensacola will depend less on your threats and more on your conduct in response to Governor Chester's proposals for dealing with the prisoners and my own concerning the city of Pensacola. We'll be sending our proposals to you tomorrow.

In the interim, I remain, Your Excellency, your most humble and obedient servant.

Pensacola General Headquarters,
March 20, 1781
John Campbell

I was happy Governor Peter Chester, with whom I had a cordial relationship before hostilities had broken out, wanted to respond to my request. Indeed, the next day, I received two letters from Chester, in one of which he made a proposal. Since he did not have adequate lodging for the Spanish prisoners in his barracks, the English were willing to let go those they might capture on their own recognizance, on humanitarian grounds, as long as they did not turn around and fight against his British Majesty or any of his allies. In another letter, the English governor agreed to protect the city's women and children from the war's calamities. He promised not to damage the city's buildings, if the Spanish troops and seamen committed no offenses nor harmed the civilian populace. On receiving these letters, I decided to ignore Campbell's impertinent terms and accept Governor Chester's proposals concerning the treatment of the prisoners of war, as well as respecting the people of Pensacola, thus avoiding using the city as a battlefield.

After analyzing all the circumstances, I concluded that it would be impossible to try to enter the main fort, Fort George, in a frontal attack. It was protected by the Queen's Fort, which my soldiers quickly dubbed the "Fort of the Half Moon," due to its elliptical shape, and Fort Prince, which dominated the hillock the English called Gage Hill. I realized I could not use the same strategy I had used successfully in the attack on other poorly defended English strongholds located in worse positions. I therefore decided to change tactics and take the time necessary to dig ample trenches and build parapets around the small enemy forts, subjecting them to a slow but steady siege, until their defenses fell like ripe fruit.

Since the terrain's steep incline would impede our troops from building ditches large enough to install our cannons there, I thought it was better to dig covered trenches around the hill in a wide perimeter so that the enemy would at no time know where exactly the soldiers were or from where they might attack.

CHAPTER 35
Dealing with the Indians
(Bernardo de Gálvez speaks)

One morning I wanted to verify with my own eyes how the trenches were coming along, so I set out to cross the bay on one of the launches. Then I climbed up the hill, careful to go the long way around and remain out of reach of the enemy artillery, which so efficiently had repelled the advance of our troops.

I had not considered that, although I was out of range of the English fort's rifles, the Indian sharpshooters hidden on the other side of the hill could still reach me. When I heard the first shot, it was already too late. I felt a burning sensation in my hand holding my command baton followed by a strong impact in my abdomen, which made me lose my balance, but I did not fall. Several men supported me while others hastened to the place where the shots had come from to punish the aggressors.

While going back across the bay, I lost consciousness for a few minutes due to blood loss, but I came to in time to get off the launch under my own power, because the news that their leader might be badly wounded could terribly demoralize the troops. The scratch on my hand was losing more blood than my belly wound, but the surgeon who gave me first aid in my tent was more concerned about the abdominal wound. Days later, he told me that I had been very lucky: the bullet had ricocheted off my cane's silver handle. If it had directly hit my abdomen, it surely would have wounded a vital organ.

When the surgeon opened my shirt to bandage me, he discovered my chest scars, the result of spear wounds. Two Indian spears had penetrated my leather body armor when alone I had chased a band of Apaches who had attacked a hacienda in Chihuahua. It was apparent that it was not the first time that I had faced the enemy alone. My wounds forced me to remain in my tent for a few days, and I used the healing time to reflect and to write details in my diary about the Pensacola campaign, thinking that at some point I would send the report to my uncle and to His Majesty. Fortunately, it was my left hand that was injured, although I could have dictated my diary to any of my aides.

That this setback had come from an Indian sharpshooter gave me pause. One of the main tasks that my uncle had set for me was to improve our relationship with the tribes in the area. This task had become more urgent after the declaration of war against England, but the preparations for the campaign had prevented me from carrying the mission out. I did find out that the military commanders of Mobile and Pensacola had first called powwows to curry favor with the Tallapoosas, Chickasaws, Choctaws and the Creeks. We were very lucky that the Indians had left there shortly before we attacked Fort Charlotte. I also found out that the Cuba Governor Diego Navarro, who had correctly foreseen the possibility that the Indians might ally with the English, had sent a schooner a few months earlier to invite the tribal chiefs to Havana, where he wined and dined them. He extracted a promise of loyalty from them, which apparently the Indians had quickly forgotten.

The ordinances that were in effect in New Spain about the conduct of the military authorities with the heathen Indians absolutely prohibited the selling of arms and liquor to them. Yet this had been exactly the principal means the other European powers had used to gain their friendship. To secure their alliance, they also distributed medals with images of their monarchs and banners so the chiefs could hang them in front of their tents. The Spanish authorities also adopted this custom when the Louisiana territory passed from French to Spanish control.

Shortly after my arrival in New Orleans, I had received a letter from Captain Fernando de Leyba, commander of the small fort at St. Louis. He warned me that he had run out of medals, banners and diplomas to distribute among the Indian chiefs and that this scarcity could provoke an incident. Leyba also stated that the chiefs of those tribes had shown a great interest in meeting me in person and that several Indian nations–the Kickapoo, Sac, Maha, Mascuten, Missouri, as well as the Great and Little Osages, had gathered in the vicinity of St. Louis for that purpose.

In his letter, Leyba himself had discouraged me from meeting them because of the high cost of such a meeting would probably incurr. He explained that once the Indians gathered en masse, there were: "only two ways of dealing with those people: either scare them off with rifle shots or feed them. As I had not been given any reason to act violently and we did not have the means to chase them away, I had no choice but to entertain them, although it cost an arm and a leg."

In the two years that the conflict between the English and the rebel colonists (whom the Indians called "Bostonians") had persisted, neither side honored their commitments with these tribes, who came to me like a puppy without a master; consequently, I had to come up with three thousand rations more than budgeted in order to feed the Indians. But when I went over the accounts, I realized that, even when war events might have cost the Spanish treasury greater expenditures in foodstuffs and gifts, the total outlay was infinitely smaller than what the Internal Provinces of New Spain had allotted to maintain the line of fortifications against Indian incursions.

Soon after returning from the Mississippi campaign, Gilbert Antoine de St. Maxent informed me that two Indian chiefs wanted to bestow on me in person several medals and other objects that they had received from the English, as proof of their rejection of the former alliance and their request to deal with Spain. To give the other tribes in the area an incentive to follow their example, I asked the intendant to bring me medals and flags so I could give them as gifts to the chieftains of the friendly tribes. I then made an appointment to meet the chiefs in the city's Plaza de Armas, ordering food and opening several carafes of alcohol to fete the chieftains.

Using Gilbert Antoine de St. Maxent as interpreter, I relayed to the chiefs his Majesty's message of great love and respect for the Indian nations in the Spanish Crown's dominions and that the Spaniards' Great Captain considered his Indian subjects the same as any other Spanish subjects. Therefore, the Great Captain fervently desired to maintain the peace with them. I then formally gave to the chiefs, who were very grateful for such gifts, two silver medals with Charles III's profile engraved on both sides and two Burgundy Cross flags.

Under the influence of alcohol, one of the chiefs pointed at one of the medals with the monarch's prominent profile and then he touched his own nose, which was just as large, guffawing at their supposed similarity. After they consumed the last morsel of meat and finished off the firewater, the chiefs left solemnly but tipsily. I went up to my office to write to my uncle in his capacity of Secretary for the Indies about the chieftains' visit.

Your Excellency. Dear Uncle:

These people are very sensitive, and it is necessary to receive them and entertain them and even put up with their impertinence, but we should not allow them to forget our superiority and the respect they must show us. I think the King will be very pleased to maintain the peace with the Indians in the region. By spending what he does in one year alone to make war on them in the Internal Provinces, he can cement peace with them for ten years.

Your faithful servant, Bernardo de Gálvez

CHAPTER 36
The Bay of Quicksilver
(Bernardo de Gálvez speaks)

I was still convalescing from my abdominal wound when, thanks to some deserters, persistent rumors circulated in the camp that Admiral George Rodney's fleet was marauding in the Caribbean. If he decided against attacking Havana, he could cross the Gulf of Mexico to help the troops under siege at Pensacola. This contingency would not have worried me if, in case of an emergency, I could trust the armada officers whose ships were already anchored in the bay.

Unfortunately, the exchange of insults and threats between Captain Calvo, the other captains and I had left deep scars among those captains, even among the ones who felt the call of honor and had asked for their leader's authorization to cross in front of the English batteries. I noted their resentment when, the day after entering the bay, I invited the principal officers of the fleet to lunch. Initially the luncheon had proceeded normally, but then an observation by one of the naval officers again set me off. Possibly I was still nervous from the tension of the prior days, and I accused the head of the armada, the Marquis González de Castejón, of having delayed the conquest of Pensacola unnecessarily. In referring to the officer collectively, I used improper language, saying that he had demonstrated his "yellow belly" in our dispute of entering the port. This elicited the protest of some captains, who begged me to change the subject. Captain Alderete, who had just entered the tent and whom I had reprimanded for not saluting me when the Galvezton passed in front of his ship after I had hoisted the flag of the admiral's joint sea and land forces, interrupted at that point. Alderete, who had always defended Captain Calvo's position, answered insolently that he had not saluted because he did not have orders to do so and naval ordinance did not require it. "Besides," he added, "nor will I ever salute you." His answer made me completely lose my temper and tell the captains they could all go back to Havana whenever they wanted because I could take Pensacola without the armada.

After the altercation, I left my tent and went for a walk on the beach, where the bay's fresh air helped me calm down. Upon my return to the camp, I sent an invitation to Alderete to dine with me and his companions on their frigate the next day. I made this gesture as a courtesy, but also because, as head of the expedition, I could not let all the commanders of the fleet turn against me. Overcoming my distaste, during the luncheon with the captains I offered to forget everything that had happened and remain on good terms with them for future operations.

I thought, perhaps naively, that the whole affair was closed, but later I found out that Alderete had reported it to his superiors and requested that the officers who had attended the first luncheon and had felt insulted give their testimony. When I heard this, I understood that the wound had not healed properly and that the ruckus with the captains would have consequences.

I was not wrong.

The surgeon who had attended to my stomach wound had not yet released me, when one night a guard brought an intercepted enemy note to my tent. The note confirmed that Admiral Rodney's fleet, composed of eight line ships and fourteen war frigates, had left for Pensacola. This was not exactly news that would help me sleep. A cold southwestern wind had begun to shake the canvas tent and made me fear that, if it were announcing a storm as on other occasions, the squadron would have to leave the narrows of the bay, meaning that the ground troops would go unprotected again.

When I tried to close my eyes, instead of falling asleep, my consciousness flashed back to the Almadén mines, when my uncle had sent me there with the charge of recovering the manuscript written by Viniegra. For some reason I've never understood, Viniegra agreed to hand over the compromising document to me voluntarily. This document had triggered his persecution by my uncle, but Viniegra knew full well that its possession was his lifeboat.

In the tent's semidarkness, the human ghosts I had encountered in the depths of the mine began to crowd in. I thought I smelled the same stench that had assaulted my senses as I descended into the mine's galleries and, above all, I remembered, as if I were reliving the scene, how Viniegra had removed the document, wrapped in a tarred cloth, from its hiding place.

"Don't think that my having hidden my account in the book of St. John was capricious on my part. In one of the scenes of the Apocalypse, one of the avenging angels breaks the seal of a great container, pouring its contents, a poisonous liquid like quicksilver, on the earth." Despite having been exposed to quicksilver for a long time, Viniegra had managed to maintain his presence of mind and had no illusions about what would befall him once he handed over the manuscript.

"Although this inferno's hardships may have been able to twist my mind," Viniegra told me, "I still have enough intelligence left to realize that this manuscript, which has created so many problems for me, has also been my safe-conduct pass. Your uncle's henchmen would never dare to kill me without knowing where the document was hidden."

After pausing for a moment, the memorialist added, "But if they decide to do it now, they will probably do me a great favor in putting me out of my misery for good."

The excitement I had felt when I had the document in my hands and Sergeant Melecio Rodríguez's rush to get on the road home had prevented me from speaking with the mine warden, whom I would have asked to free Viniegra after he handed over the document for which he had been persecuted and imprisoned. I dared not intercede on his behalf with my uncle José when he received me in his office. I could not overlook that in exchange for my having retrieved Viniegra's manuscript, my uncle was giving me a decree of appointment as colonel of the Standing Regiment and future governor of Louisiana. It was true that my life had unfolded in such a way that, since taking on my new post and its pressing responsibilities, that even if I had wanted to, it would have been impossible to verify from the other end of the Earth what Viniegra's fate had been.

In any case, since I was loath to continue sharing my tent with the mine ghosts, I got up out of bed and got dressed, being careful not to make any sudden moves that could reopen my stomach wound. So as not to wake my aide sleeping in the next tent, I tiptoed out very slowly. The sound of my footsteps was muffled by the sand that the wind had swept into the camp. When I arrived at the camp's perimeter, the sentinels recognized my silhouette, perhaps because I limped slightly, as a result of the injury, and they let me pass without asking me for the password. After sweeping the clouds from the firmament, the southwest wind had lessened, so that when I arrived at the bay shore, I found the sea completely becalmed.

A silvery moon illuminated the landscape, which reminded me of the view of the great river that I had contemplated from the port of New Orleans for the first time also on a moonlit night. In the moonlight, the bay's expanse reminded me of the consistency of the huge quicksilver pool I had seen in the Almadén mines.

CHAPTER 37
Unexpected Help

Bernardo de Gálvez had barely returned from his evening stroll when an aide arrived at his tent with the message that ship sails had been seen headed for Punta Sigüenza on the other side of Santa Rosa Island. Forgetting completely about his wound and barely wrapping himself in his cape, Gálvez ran up the hill to observe the tip of the island and the Red Cliffs. At dawn, the drifting fog had not yet lifted on the coast, so Gálvez could not see through his spyglass the flags flying on the ships or any other signs that would identify their nationality. When the mist began to clear, however, he recognized the red and yellow flag on the poop deck of one of the ships. The Royal Spanish Navy had established a new insignia by ordinance to avoid having the white and blue flag of St. Andrew's Cross confused with the deep blue sea. He soon verified that all the ships on the horizon were Spanish.

Gálvez could not understand how the British fleet he had expected to arrive had turned into a Spanish fleet before his eyes, as if by magic. He did not have to wait too long to find out, because a midshipman delivered a letter to him from a launch sent from the San Luis sailing ship that had just tied up at the dock on the bay's inner shore. It read:

Dear Sir,

According to reports we've received from Cape Corrientes indicating an enemy squadron has passed by there, the council has resolved that, suspecting it might be heavy reinforcements heading for Pensacola, his Majesty's squadron, under the command of Squadron Leader José Solano, and a detail of one thousand six hundred troops under my orders should leave immediately to take care of anything that might occur in those parts.

In the letter signed by the commander of the army, Juan Manuel Cajigal, he mentioned the availability of another one thousand three hundred and fifty men that Solano could make available, including additional reinforcements from the ships under French Squadron Commander Chevalier de Monteil, who had joined the Spanish fleet.

As a reward for his victory at Pensacola, King Carlos III had appointed Gálvez as Field Marshal. In addition to the immense satisfaction Marshal Gálvez felt, he appreciated the personal note in the postscript to Cajigal's letter even more:

My Dear Friend,

I am here at your service whenever you see fit to call upon me. You know how much I esteem I have for you and how similar our way of thinking is. When next I see you, I'll tell you what happened during our famous council meeting and what I think about current events.

Your obedient servant and loyal friend, Cajigal

That same night, Gálvez invited Cajigal, his son and two aides to his table at the camp. One of the aides was the Venezuelan lieutenant, Francisco de Miranda. Gálvez used his convalescence as an excuse not to observe protocol by inviting the other military officers, especially those from the armada. Commander Cajigal was the son of the former captain general of Cuba and, as a member of the War Council in Havana, had always supported Gálvez's requests for reinforcements. According to the postscript promising to update Gálvez on what had happened at the "famous meeting," Gálvez already imagined Cajigal would provide him with some juicy gossip. Cajigal knew about the rift between Gálvez and the armada captains, because the San Ramón had carried the news to Cuba on its return without the rest of the squadron.

During dinner, with the wine flowing bottle after bottle from Gilbert Antoine de St. Maxent' wine cellar, Cajigal provided the information he had hinted at in his letter about why the captain general of Cuba had sent the fleet to support the Spanish troops in Pensacola. The British admiralty knew that Cuba was the key to the Spanish defense in the Caribbean and dispatched Rodney's fleet to invade Havana once again. But since the last invasion, the Spanish authorities had reinforced the port city's defenses and marked its perimeter with buoys and patrol boats; on land brigades of troops and munitions were ready to move quickly by mule transport. They reinforced El Morro and built another fort. The bitter experience of the brief British occupation had subsequently resulted in the capital city becoming the most militarized in the Caribbean.

Admiral Rodney carried out a lengthy inspection around the island of Cuba and concluded that any act of aggression would be very dangerous. He, therefore, dared only land on the town of Jaruco's beach and sacked some farms in the area. The footprint Rodney left in Cuba on that occasion more closely resembled that of a common buccaneer than that of the most important commander of the British fleet in the Caribbean. Rodney set his ships on a northwest course, which Captain General Navarro interpreted as a diversionary tactic intended to disguise Rodney's real mission of bringing relief to the English troops under siege at Pensacola. Thus, Navarro decided to send Solano's flotilla and Cajigal's troops to reinforce the Spanish soldiers who had already landed on Santa Rosa Island.

Gálvez and Cajigal took advantage of their first encounter to refine their plan for joint action against Pensacola. The two commanders were friends and comrades in arms, and their soirée with other officers in attendance lasted into the wee hours, each of them recounting anecdotes and tales that made the other officers in attendance applaud and laugh long and hard. Francisco de Miranda, who at first seemed a bit inhibited perhaps because he was the only Creole officer in the group, opened towards the end of the evening by relating how a war ship's chaplain had subjected an admiral to a stiff penance after he discovered a book banned by the Inquisition in his cabin. According to Miranda, the priest in exercising his ecclesiastic prerogative had forced his superior in the armada to carry out an act of public penance: crawling on his knees up a gravelly hill to a shrine near Havana with his waistcoat tucked up and a piece of sail and rigging on his shoulder as if it were a cross.

Although all those present laughed heartily at the story, they didn't all know who it was that had carried out the chaplain's order and shown his behind in public. It was none other than the commander-in-chief of the fleet himself, who had just arrived at the coast of Pensacola: General José Solano.

CHAPTER 38
Incident in the Trenches
(Bernardo de Gálvez speaks)

Admiral Rodney's fleet had not yet turned up near Pensacola, and we were thankful for the presence of General Solano's fleet protecting the port's estuary against the possible incursion of the British fleet. The general had offered me his complete support in the taking of the forts, placing at my disposal some of his gunners and a couple companies of midshipmen. With the reinforcements Cajigal brought, I probably would not need Solano's men to defeat the English forts. I nevertheless accepted General Solano's and Cajigal's offer so that his men could share in the glory of the victory.

The fact was I had already drawn three thousand men from the militias and from among the black population and had incorporated them into the professional troops, even before Solana's and Cajigal's arrival. If to this number were added the recently arrived reinforcements, which rose to some one thousand five hundred in addition to the French admiral's troops, the number of soldiers under my command totaled nearly eight thousand, which topped my most ambitious requests when I had begun to organize the expedition to Pensacola from New Orleans.

I was wary of the overconfidence and lax discipline we might experience because of this numeric superiority with respect to the English troops defending the city's stronghold. It would be difficult to find another explanation for the regrettable incident that happened in the trenches after the engineers had succeeded in installing six 24-inch cannons on the hilltop.

Around noon, I was meeting with several military leaders in my tent, when we were interrupted by a loud artillery explosion coming from the Half Moon Fort, followed by a hail of bullets. When my men came to give me the news, they said the English had attacked from that fort, completely surprising our sentinels, who were not expecting such a move from the fort's defenders. The fact was that by taking advantage of our carelessness, the English had attacked the trenches with impunity, destroying everything they could and carrying off everything they found in their path, including the silverware from the commander's dining room table. In the process, they bayonetted unarmed soldiers, who vomited blood from their lungs as well as their not-yet-digested lunch. Then, before returning to their stronghold, they spiked the cannons that had not yet been used to batter their defenses.

Taken by surprise, the Mallorca Regiment dragoons ran towards the enemy lines shouting, "We're done for. They're putting us to the sword!" So the attackers made a royal hash of those cowards: eighteen dead and sixteen wounded. The English also took a very high number of prisoners, among them the captain of the Hibernia Regiment. The obvious conclusion I drew after the first reports came in was that the English attack would not have been so bad if those in charge had been attending to their duties. I ordered the immediate arrest of Captain Pablo Figuerola, who was commander of the trenches, and charged him as responsible for the setback and death of his soldiers.

In addition to the irreparable loss of human life and serious material damage, an incident like this contributed to undermining the morale of an army that perhaps was too confident of victory. The fact was that most of the troops had not experienced combat. All they had were skirmishes with British artillery and some surprise Indian attacks in the woods on the outskirts of the city.

While we were seated drinking refreshments that very afternoon in my tent, Francisco de Miranda cursed the unfortunate affair: "Before this mishap happened, I noticed the way the trenches had been dug. They looked more like holes in the ground. As far as their superiors were concerned, some of the soldiers commented to me that at the time of the attack, they were unprepared, enjoying a hearty lunch as if instead of being on the battlefield, they were lunching at an inn on the Plaza Mayor in Madrid."

"Those trenches," I answered Miranda somewhat brusquely, "have been dug in the best way possible, considering the terrain's poor quality and their proximity to enemy lines. As far as the commanders' behavior during the incident, we should wait for the result of the court martial I have ordered for those responsible, out of respect for military justice."

In trying to change the subject, we ran into another topic Miranda and I could not agree on: the English deploying Indian soldiers, who were happy to torture the enemies they captured alive. Miranda expressed his admiration for General Campbell, who the day before had saved a poor Spanish prisoner from death at the hands of Indians by exchanging the captive for the exorbitant ransom of two hundred *pesos* and several kegs of rum.

"Actually," added Miranda, "this kind of excess is characteristic of those uncivilized savages, while the English general's humanitarian gesture demonstrates, in contrast, the concern civilized people have for their brethren."

"My experiences in fighting on the frontier of New Spain for several years forces me to disagree with your interpretation of the different levels of civilization between the white man and the 'savages,' as you call them, although I prefer to call them Indians," I countered. "We are in complete agreement in thinking that the Indian soldiers' behavior with their prisoners is deplorable, although I believe that to understand their stance rightly, we would have to analyze the treatment they have received at the hands of the white man, too. Perhaps it would surprise you to know that some of their worst habits, like scalping their enemies, they learned from us, when we put a price on their heads."

It was not easy to convince Miranda, who responded to my argument, "Doubtless your Excellency has much greater experience than I in dealing with the savages, but you must agree that General Campbell's gesture of rescuing one of our men from the hands of the savages demonstrates his humanitarian quality."

"As far as the English general's character is concerned, I also cast doubt on his respect for human life, because when we were negotiating the terms of the campaign, I had to convince Campbell not to destroy city buildings just because they were in the way of his cannons."

"I wasn't aware of that detail, since I wasn't here at the beginning of the siege."

"Let me also mention that I haven't heard positive reports about the Englishman's civilized and humanitarian behavior towards the natives of the region. When the English want to possess Indian-occupied territory, they have no qualms in running them off their lands and exterminating them, sometimes using such repulsive methods as distributing smallpox-infected blankets."

At that moment, Cajigal noticed that my discussion with Miranda was becoming heated, so he made up an excuse to send Miranda on an errand.

When we were alone in the tent, I commented to the commander, "It's apparent this aide of yours has a talent for debate, although perhaps due to his youth he may fall into the mistake of speaking forcefully about topics he knows nothing about."

"Of course, all of us make mistakes," replied Cajigal, "but I must say that, in general, Miranda has judged many situations correctly, based on his outstanding cultural knowledge. The man feels a true passion for books and travels with them everywhere. He absorbs their content at the drop of a hat. In truth, Miranda is a walking library."

"Maybe it would be a good idea for him to add to his library a manual on the opportunity to remain silent under certain circumstances," I said. "For example, I think his derisive comments about what happened in the trenches were out of line, when the bodies of the soldiers who died in that unfortunate incident have not yet grown cold."

CHAPTER 39
The Half Moon Fort Explosion

(Bernardo de Gálvez speaks)

That same afternoon, a strong southeastern wind arose that unleashed storm clouds on the coast, some of which lingered on top of the Red Cliffs like a huge turban. As the day wore on, the storm escalated with strong wind gusts that in some places whipped up sand devils and shook the camp's tents so much that it seemed as though they were going to take flight. Having survived other thrashings by the elements, I knew that when the sky began to cloud over like that, the storm was going to get worse. I therefore gave instructions to the ship captains, whose vessels were anchored in the bay, to unmoor them and head for the open sea.

The clouds had barely crossed the port's estuary, when the bay waters became so choppy that it seemed as if a terrible combat between sea monsters had been unleashed at the bottom of the bay. On the other side of the bay, sheets of water were falling on the hill that the English strongholds occupied. I feared a flash flood would swamp our trenches, which is exactly what happened. The downpour also completely flooded the hospital tent, and gusts of wind tore out the tent stakes from the sand, leaving the sick and wounded men exposed to the rain. I myself went to the hospital to help, but I could not prevent some of the patients, probably taken aback by the plethora of thunderclaps and lightning, from dying of fright.

While I was helping one of my men secure a tent's stakes, I slipped on the wet sand and, as I fell like a sack of potatoes, I felt a tearing in my stomach. I had reopened my wound. When the surgeon removed the bandage, he discovered the wound had begun to bleed again. That night, I had to remain in my tent, lying on my cot with damp blankets, the torn canvas allowing the wind to blow through the tent.

Even under those conditions, my exhaustion from the past few days was such that sleep overcame me. I had a dream that turned into a horrible nightmare. I was again on board the Galvezton at the foot of the Red Cliffs, leading a small fleet of war ships that was attempting to bombard the English batteries on top of the cliffs. Although no one in his right mind would try to take the enemy stronghold by sea, I had given orders to a company of midshipmen to land at the foot of the rocks and attempt to scale the promontory to the top. One of my men dared to point out to me, "Commander, this battle is folly because our cannons can never reach the fort's height, and the troops can't climb the rock face that has a sheer drop almost straight down to the water." I threatened to run him through with my sword if he did not follow my instructions to order his midshipmen to land immediately at the bottom of the cliff and attempt the climb. Although the officer knew he was ordering his men to a sure death, he gave them the order to climb the rock face. Then the dream showed me a cloud of gunpowder obscuring the promontory's vertical surface, it seemed so real, to the point of making me believe that I was inhaling the acrid smell of gunpowder. When the smoke cleared away, I looked through the spyglass at those who had managed to climb half way up the cliffs. I realized they weren't human soldiers, but a platoon of apes dressed in the uniforms of midshipmen. While they climbed the rock face, they made gestures typical of those animals, although their eyes were as wide as saucers mirroring a very human terror. Afterwards, a barrage came from the promontory batteries, and I saw that the apes had been completely blown away by the shrapnel, their disjointed bodies fallen into the water like rag dolls.

That vision was so real, I woke up just before dawn. After squeezing the blood and water from the bandage on my wound, I left the tent–or what was left of it after the gale—to see with my own eyes how the storm had ravaged the camp. The same as I had done in days past, I headed along the shore, which the heavy sea had strewn with seaweed and seashells. I went to a place where I could observe the forts on the other side of the bay and the perimeter of our trenches. During the night, the engineer-sappers had managed to reduce the water that at one point was running through the trenches like a torrent down a mountainside. I confirmed our batteries would continue to function, because when the sun arose in a red ball of fire, the Spanish artillery cannons boomed. The Half Moon Fort, which was the closest to our trenches, promptly responded.

I was on my way back to the camp, when the whole bay basin echoed a tremendous explosion, whose shockwave I felt on my back. When I turned around, I managed to see that one of the smaller English outposts, which I identified as the Half Moon Fort because of its position, had just blown up. The explosion had thrust into the sky an immense column of smoke that blotted out the sun and spread helter-skelter a hail of wall fragments, pieces of copper and even the disarticulated, broken bodies of soldiers had been blown up into the sky as if they were marionettes.

I had hardly returned to my tent, when one of the captains of the trenches, who had crossed the bay rapidly in a launch, told me that one of the grenades thrown from our trenches had hit the Half-Moon Fort's munitions dump, blowing apart the entire stronghold and causing heavy casualties among those taking cover behind those walls.

To take maximum advantage of that trump card that luck had dealt us, I rapidly gave instructions to Cajigal and the other commanders to have their troops attack the crippled fort immediately and drive out the English soldiers still on site. My orders were obeyed forthwith, and Cajigal's, José de Espeleta's and Jerónimo de Girón's troops rose to attack from the trenches. The surviving English soldiers, perhaps for fear of being hit by our bullets if they risked retreating towards Fort George, took cover among the rubble, like crabs surprised by the tide. It was not easy to extract them from there.

Despite the favorable circumstances, which I wanted to exploit, Captain Alderete committed yet another act of insubordination when, in following my instructions, Cajigal delivered a note to Alderete that read, "Dear Sir, Field Marshal Gálvez has instructed me to tell you that in view of our enemies being found with their exterior walls ruined and given his Majesty's troops have secured them, please attack the main fort in that part of the bay, Fort George, immediately by any means you see fit and with all the vessels you think necessary to achieve victory."

Alderete knew perfectly well that Cajigal was only conveying my instructions, but in his absurd insistence on protocol, which apparently concerned him more than service to the King, Alderete did not carry out my instructions to attack Fort George from the shore. In the end, it turned out our ships' barrage on Fort George was not necessary to convince General Campbell that the moment had arrived to hoist the white flag, something he was probably looking forward to since the beginning of the siege. Espeleta, who received a superficial wound, and Cajigal, who suffered a concussion during the attack, had barely taken possession of the Half Moon Fort, when a flag announcing a ceasefire could be seen waving over Fort George.

A messenger from Campbell handed me this note: "Sir: To avoid more bloodshed, I propose to Your Excellency a ceasefire until tomorrow at midday, during which time I will study the Articles of Capitulation. I assume Your Excellency is willing to agree to honorable terms for the troops under my command, as well as ensuring the defense, security and protection of the civilians."

I was already familiar with General Campbell's tricks, so I rejected the document, which could be a decoy in order to allow the English to regroup their forces. Instead, I demanded talks to discuss surrender begin immediately, which the Englishman accepted.

Given the complexity and importance of the terms, the writing of the document lasted all night and did not conclude until later the next morning. During the drafting of the terms of surrender, James Campbell, the general's nephew, participated with full authority. I did not know how to interpret this: whether it was an attempt to expedite matters or a new rebuff by the arrogant Scottish aristocrat. On the Spanish side, I wanted Colonel Ezpeleta, who had felt disappointed by the outcomes the English had drawn from the generous terms of surrender in Mobile, to be involved directly in the writing of the documents.

Once the documents were signed by representatives of each side, the surrender of Fort George proceeded. With all military honors, General Campbell and another nine hundred soldiers paraded with their rifles at their shoulders and their flags waving in front of our victorious troops. Then they surrendered their arms and their flags while our cannons fired artillery salvos to celebrate the event.

Once we had access to the forts that had withstood the explosion, we discovered a surprising war booty of more than one hundred and forty cannons, two thousand one hundred rifles, three hundred barrels of gunpowder and miscellaneous military supplies. I could not help but think that, if Campbell had had the guts, his troops could have withstood a much longer siege without running out of arms or supplies, and that therefore the letter addressed to General Clinton that we had intercepted had not reflected the true situation.

As if General Campbell wanted to prove his bad faith once more, he took advantage on the very evening we were negotiating the surrender by having three hundred dragoons leave the fort for Georgia under cover of night, thereby diminishing the number of British troops who would become prisoners of war. The English also distributed abundant rations of gunpowder and firewater among their Indian allies that night. Thus, after perpetrating many acts of cruelty, the Indians returned to their villages with significant booty, which included the scalps of many Spanish soldiers.

The surrender ceremony had scarcely ended, when I sent one message on the brigantine Galvezton to the governor de Cuba and another to my uncle, Secretary for the Indies. With my own script, I announced to them that I had completed the difficult mission that His Majesty had entrusted to me: to drive the English from their positions on the Mississippi River and from the towns on the Gulf of Mexico. When the news of our victory reached Spain, the euphoria and gratitude that burst out in the Court almost surpassed the rain of ashes and debris that had resulted when the Half Moon Fort's arsenal blew up in Pensacola.

This time, what fell upon us from the sky were the many mercies and promotions his Majesty the King conceded to reward those of us who had contributed to the triumph of our arms. The campaign commanders, Solano, Cajigal and I myself were promoted to lieutenant generals; Ezpeleta and Girón were made brigadiers; and this shower of military rewards reached also the subordinate ranks.

In addition to being promoted to colonel, Francisco de Miranda also reaped the booty of two black slaves, Bob and Perth, acquired for four hundred ninety dollars. He also obtained an interesting collection of books in English from the Pensacola bookstore of John Falconer & Company, which included works by Chesterfield, Watson *(The Reign of Philip II)* and Robertson *(History of Scotland),* and poetry by Milton and Waller.

Part Five

CHAPTER 40
Prince Castle

After the promotions given by his Majesty the King to the military and naval commanders who had participated in the taking of Pensacola, Bernardo de Gálvez received his appointment as chief of joint operations in the Bahamas for the conquest of Jamaica, while retaining his titles of governor of Louisiana and Western Florida. Admiral Solano became the commander of the armada in Havana, replacing Admiral Juan Bonet, with whom Gálvez had had serious run-ins during the meetings of the War Council. Juan Manuel Cajigal was appointed captain general and governor of Cuba, replacing Diego Navarro, who had not seen eye to eye with Gálvez either.

Shortly after Juan Manuel Cajigal returned from West Florida, he had barely assumed his posting as governor of Cuba, when an unpleasant incident occurred. None other than General John Campbell himself stopped over in Havana en route to New York on the Spanish flag-of-truce war ship carrying the prisoners of war who had surrendered in Pensacola.

Perhaps the Spanish Governor Cajigal's excessive sense of courtesy prompted him to receive his vanquished adversary with a reassuring pat on the back, as in Diego Velázquez's painting "The Surrender at Breda." When he found out that Campbell had landed at El Morro castle, he immediately sent an invitation to the English general and his officers, who were accompanying him on his ship, to have lunch with him at his magnificent residence. It would have been natural for Francisco de Miranda, who was one of the few officers close to the new governor who spoke adequate English to be invited to this luncheon to serve as interpreter for Cajigal and the British officers. But Miranda had left the city to spend a few days at the Count of Casa Montalvo's hacienda to recover from a high fever. Cajigal therefore designated another of his aides, one José de Montesinos who only spoke French, to communicate with the single British officer who could speak French. A problem ensued at the end of the reception at the governor's palace, when Cajigal offered his guests a carriage tour of the city and Montesinos committed the faux-pas of taking the British prisoners of war to visit the Prince Castle military installation, which was contrary to the most elemental precautions.

It was the fort the Cuban authorities had recently built in a distant location from the other Spanish fortifications that had been used in vain to prevent the English from occupying Havana in 1762. Exploiting the location of an old tumbled-down tower, Brigadier Louis Huet had completed the new fort and named it Prince Castle in honor of the future King of Spain, Charles IV. It was a modern fortress incorporating the latest techniques in military construction.

While still at war, the military authorities in Havana had indiscreetly shown the English officers one of the city's defensive strongholds; this transgressed every military code. Was it a huge breakdown in military security? Or perhaps the Spaniards had taken the English officers to Prince Castle specifically to show them that, after the English occupation, the city's defenses had been so reinforced that it would now be absurd to attempt a new assault?

Given that General Campbell's character was rather unpredictable, it was even more difficult to guess what was going through his mind. He had just lost a strategic town of essential value for the British fleet and army. To a certain extent, the taking of Pensacola by Gálvez had been payback for the earlier English occupation of Havana. Was Campbell offended that the Spaniards were subtly rubbing his nose in his defeat?

The man who definitively not only felt offended, but who screamed bloody murder was Brigadier Louis Huet. He felt justifiably proud of having used his up-to-date knowledge of defense in Prince Castle's construction. When he found out that General Campbell and other British officers had been permitted to visit the fort and tour its installations, he immediately sent a letter to the officer who was on duty that day at Prince Castle to demand an explanation as to why General Campbell had been permitted to reconnoiter the installation "at his leisure."

In his reply to Huet, the officer on duty underplayed the importance of the visit, saying he had not even realized they were foreign visitors. Campbell and his officers were not wearing uniforms. He had granted limited access to the fort to those accompanied by one of the captain general's aides, adding in an attempt to extricate himself, that the foreigners only saw the interior and nothing of the exterior, which was apparently illogical.

Given this less than satisfactory answer, Brigadier Huet passed a copy of his correspondence to Captain General Cajigal, who wanted to play down the incident, although he upbraided the officer on duty. Cajigal must have felt responsible in part for not having given sufficiently clear instructions to the officer charged with accompanying the Englishmen during their visit to the city's outskirts. Be that as it may, the Secretary for the Indies José de Gálvez came to hear of the incident and asked the military authorities to carry out a timely investigation about this breakdown in security and to have the guilty party punished. Whether it was due to bad faith or to simple ignorance of what had really happened that day, Francisco de Miranda was blamed.

Once this unfounded accusation was put into circulation, in no time Cajigal himself received a letter from Secretary José de Gálvez informing him that the King himself was highly displeased with the news that General Campbell and other officers had been allowed to see the town's fortifications. The Gálvez's letter specified, "… under the influence and in the company of Don Francisco de Miranda, who is an anglophile." In that same letter, José Gálvez also transmitted his Majesty's command for Cajigal to remove Miranda from his side immediately and put him on the first boat out of Havana. For all intents and purposes, Miranda would be banished from the Spanish empire.

Governor Cajigal was aware of the Secretary of the Indies' almost unlimited power but did not attach too much importance to the letter and did not carry out the order to arrest Miranda, his admired aide, who was dear to him. Cajigal knew the accusation was false, because Miranda was out of town when the incident took place.

In his reply to the Secretary José Gálvez, Cajigal explained that Miranda could not have accompanied Campbell to Prince Castle because on that day he was far from Havana at a farm called Ojo de Agua owned by the Count of Casa Montalvo. There were several witnesses willing to corroborate those facts. Given that the English layover in Havana had been very brief, Colonel Miranda and General Campbell had not even crossed paths in the city. Cajigal concluded his letter, stating that any action taken against his aide based on these unfounded accusations would be an abuse and an injustice.

Neither Juan Manuel de Cajigal nor Francisco de Miranda understood at the time that they had put into motion a ticking time bomb, which would later detonate and damage not only Miranda's future but his protector's as well.

CHAPTER 41
The Republican Virtue of Sarah Livingston

Once Spain had declared war on England, the United States Congress designated John Jay, who up until then had presided over that legislative body, to represent his country at Charles III's court. Jay's wife, Sarah Livingston did not hesitate even a moment to accompany her husband on this difficult mission. Sarah knew very well that her husband's apparently impressive appointment as ambassador came amid the unsettled relationship of the Spanish monarchy to the new United States was evolving. The English colonies in New England were still fighting for independence and official recognition by other nations. Sarah was perfectly familiar with how the Spanish court had behaved ambiguously from the beginning of the conflict and knew how one of the congressional commissioners had been arrested, as if he were a common criminal, while trying to get to Madrid. Although she was willing to support her husband no matter what, Sarah was worried that John Jay, who had had a brilliant legal political career, would be ignored by the country's rulers. From the start, she felt no affinity for the people around her.

Sarah was imbued with the ideals of Republican virtue and firmly believed in the necessity of sacrificing personal interest in the name of the common good. In that spirit, she decided to accompany her husband on the long and risky trip and, above all, bear the pain of separation from her eldest son, Peter Augustus. Sarah was convinced that a Republican woman's duty was always to support her husband, providing him tranquility in his private life so that he could fulfill his public commitment. Many of the revolutionary leaders were aware of her sacrifice. Among them was General Washington himself, who was a friend of her father's, William Livingstone. A little before their departure, Washington sent her a letter with a very personal gift, a lock of his own hair: "I am pleased to leave you this small gift and ardently desire you favorable winds, pleasant sailing, and may all good things smooth the path you are about to embark upon."

Unfortunately, the commander-in-chief of the Continental Army could not extend his power to the elements. The American frigate Confederation carrying the Jays along with other members of the diplomatic entourage to Spain encountered rough waters during the crossing, according to Sarah's letter to her mother: "Around four in the morning, we were alarmed by a tremendous crash coming from the deck. . . . The main mast had tipped over. . . . Imagine, Mother, what a dangerous situation, more than three hundred souls, left to their fate in the vastness of the ocean on a vessel without a mast and no steering capability."

Fortunately, the Jays' precarious situation did not last long. The French frigate Aurore came to their rescue. When they arrived at the port of Cádiz, Commander Antonio de Gálvez, who was the Secretary for the Indies José de Gálvez's brother, placed a landing craft at their service to transfer them by sea to the port of Santa María.

After the less than pleasant experience Sarah had had on the high seas, the traveler commented on the delights of smooth sailing across the Bay of Cádiz in another of her letters: "The cabin was decorated with a red damask canopy with delightful fringe and the benches had cushions covered in the same fabric. There were sixteen or twenty oarsmen who wore an extravagant but not disagreeable uniform. . . . The rhythmic sound of the oars, the music, the good weather, and the beautiful panorama of the bay worked together to make the crossing truly pleasant."

After the long crossing they waited for the court in Madrid to make a welcoming gesture and recognize John Jay. Then the couple decided to stay a while to enjoy the radiance and the hospitality of the city of Cádiz. There, they had the good fortune of finding Hortensia Ortiz, who had been in service to the British consul and had

learned enough English to become their interpreter, given that neither Sarah nor John could speak a word of Spanish.

In Cádiz, John Jay waited a long time for Madrid to send a word
of welcome or to acknowledge him as a United States government
representative. Finally, tired of waiting, he decided to go to Madrid,
accompanied by Sarah and the rest of their entourage. Before leaving they had been warned about the harshness of Spanish roads, but
Sarah was unprepared for how uncomfortable the carriages were, for
the coachmen's unkempt look and above all for the filthiness of the
inns.

Fortunately, the diligent and obliging Hortensia tried to help her
new employers avoid all the discomforts she could. In her broken
English and Andalusian Spanish dialect, she became their interpreter. Without her, the Americans would have been even more lost
in the first months of their stay in Spain. Hortensia had gotten to
know the carter Martín Porres, who previously had transported
quicksilver ore from the Almadén mines to the port of Cádiz. Thus,
he knew the way well. Despite his somewhat ominous appearance,
he related with a certain wit the anecdotes he had accumulated during his previous trips.

Martin also wove harrowing tales about bandits assaulting travelers along those same roads, but Hortensia preferred not to translate
those particular tales for the American visitors, who were already
worried about the stories they had read about English travelers in
Andalusia. On arriving in the vicinity of Almadén, Martín told the
travelers how work was done in the mines that produced the quicksilver necessary for amalgamating gold and silver in the mines of
Spain's American colonies. In passing, he attempted to impress the
foreigners with some shocking details about mining work, such as
the fact that hard-labor prisoners were condemned to live without
sunlight and suffer the harsh extraction process for cinnabar, whose
effluvia produced lethal effects. He even ended the story with the
tale of a horrible fire that had ravaged the mine a few years back, a
fire that possibly had been set by the prisoners themselves. Many
miners had died when the flames spread through the galleries and
blocked the exit.

When the Jays finally arrived in Madrid, they had the luck of finding the same house on San Mateo Street that had belonged to the British ambassador before war was declared. The neighborhood was very pleasant, and the house featured a source of potable water in the garden, which allowed its residents to avoid depending on the water-sellers to fill their cisterns. What's more, Hortensia's experience in other Englishmen's homes helped Sarah to adapt to that dwelling, which in a few days the diligent servant had made sparkle like gold, with a sense of cleanliness more appropriate to southern Andalusian Spaniards than to northern Castilians.

"Señora, here the dirt is taking over!" Hortensia had said before hiking up her skirts and kneeling to scrub the floor, whose tiles she left so clean you could almost eat off them.

The satisfaction of their having arrived at their destination and finding suitable living quarters faded, however, when John Jay was confronted with the unpleasant reality that the Count of Floridablanca would not receive him. Similarly, King Charles III would not accept his credentials, he was reluctant to recognize the American congressional delegates as representatives of a sovereign nation.

The lack of official recognition complicated the mission that had brought John Jay to Spain and put his wife in the uncomfortable position of being ostracized socially. Back home, the Livingstones belonged to the economic and intellectual elite, and Sarah was accustomed to attending many social events and meeting with other women who helped each other through the rigors and the hardships of war. Sarah not only missed her son and the rest of his family, she missed contact with other people of her class.

"Here we are in a country whose customs, language and religion are absolutely contrary to ours. With no social ties, no friends: judge then if God couldn't have prepared a more acceptable destiny for us," wrote Sarah to her sister, after having lived a few months in Madrid. As time passed, Sarah found it unconscionable that her husband, who enjoyed greater prestige and acceptance in the new American society, was snubbed by the Spanish government. When the secretary of state and the King would not receive him, it made it very difficult for Jay to convey the instructions he had received from Congress.

The couple's economic difficulties added to Jay's frustration. Congress had not sent him money, and the loan that Benjamin Franklin had given him upon his arrival ran out quickly, especially because the Spanish capital was one of Europe's most expensive cities. The court and the government constantly changed location from Madrid to Aranjuez, and from there to La Granja and El Escorial. Anyone who wanted to be received at Court had to go to those places and cover the resulting extra expenses. "It costs ten dollars every time a carriage pulled by a mule team takes me from here to Aranjuez (a distance of seven leagues)," Jay complained bitterly in a letter to one of his brothers-in-law, "and my situation is so precarious I cannot pay a courier to take my dispatches to the coast or to France."

CHAPTER 42
Guarico Island

Having been appointed chief of allied operations in the Bahamas for the conquest of Jamaica, Bernardo de Gálvez was posted to the island of Guarico, where the Spanish and French military and naval forces had agreed to meet before embarking on the campaign against the British bastion, which continued to be the key to British activity in the Caribbean.

En route to their destination, they had spent a long stopover in Cuba, where Bernardo and Felicitas, who was in the last months of pregnancy, made the most of the stop to officially marry—despite their having already been wed in secret. With all due ecclesiastic and civil canons respected, Bishop Santiago José de Echevarría y Elguera officiated at the wedding celebrated in Santiago de Cuba's cathedral. Don Miguel Antonio Herrera y Chacón and the widow Countess of Macurijes were the best man and matron of honor.

They had already arrived on Guarico Island when Felicitas gave birth to their son Miguel, which was a cause for immense pride and satisfaction for Gálvez. The preparations for the baptism promised a splendid and solemn affair. An honor guard composed of armed grenadiers and French soldiers accompanied the newborn to the church in a procession. So many people gathered around the temple that the troops had to make their way through the crowd to carry the child into the baptistery. At the moment of the christening, as well as upon leaving the church, salvos of artillery were fired, which were perhaps meant to herald a brilliant military career for the child, like his father's. (The neophyte himself was baptized by the regimental chaplain of Guadalajara;

his parents had dressed him in a tiny grenadier uniform as a symbolic offering to the King from the father of a first-born son.)

At their residence, Felicitas and Bernardo held a reception for six hundred Spanish and French soldiers and provided refreshments for another two hundred invited guests. This was followed by musical entertainment and dancing and topped off with a magnificent dinner.

As a soldier used to action, Gálvez was not accustomed to wait more on the decisions of people in other parts of the globe than on his own initiative. As time passed, waiting became even more unbearable. He accepted the situation, however, anticipating dazzling success when he succeeded in assembling the critical number of ships and troops to make the taking of Jamaica possible. But Bernardo de Gálvez had to put up with the wait for years. Nevertheless, he swallowed the bitter pill of inaction the same way he had put up with difficult circumstances at other times.

On the other hand, for Felicitas de St. Maxent, the time they lived in the Guarico Island paradise was one of the happiest of her life. She enjoyed the company of her husband, whom she had missed during the long Pensacola campaign, and took delight in caring for their newborn son. Other than caring for her family and helping her husband contain his justified impatience, Felicitas did not have taxing responsibilities or obligations. She often dedicated her time to long rides in a trap drawn by two spirited horses that she herself drove, sometimes taking the children with her and at other times accompanied by a French officer who entertained her with conversation in the language she knew best.

Gálvez spent his time keeping order and harmony among the Spanish and French officers, who sometimes quarreled over nothing and could challenge each other to duels. He also was busy maintaining active correspondence with various authorities in Europe and in the Americas. The proximity of the island of Cuba also gave him some work to do, as Captain General Juan Manuel de Cajigal and Francisco de Miranda never missed a chance to get involved in some intrigue or another.

Cajigal had not received any response to his letter defending his aide from the accusation of misconduct in the matter of General Campbell's visit to Havana. Indeed, Governor Cajigal thought the affair was closed. That is why, given his commanding officer's support, Cajigal thought the moment had come to undertake new projects.

The war between Spain and England had now lasted several years, and had brought hundreds of English prisoners to Cuba, thus overflowing the jail cells and provoking an untenable situation. On the island of Jamaica, the English had their own similar problems, with Spanish prisoners overcrowding their jails. It occurred to Francisco de Miranda, and Cajigal supported him, that the military authorities of both nations could agree to exchange prisoners; it would not only be a humanitarian gesture but would also save the treasuries of London and Madrid a considerable amount of money.

Cajigal, thus, proposed that Gálvez make an overture to the English authorities in Jamaica and commission Colonel Miranda, who spoke fluent English, to venture to Jamaica with the purpose of discussing an agreement to exchange the prisoners, adding espionage as a complement to Miranda mission. Miranda would verify the military situation of the island, the state of its defenses, ports and garrisons, as well as determining the best way to carry out an attack.

Although Gálvez recognized Miranda's superior intellect, he did not have Cajigal's confidence in the Venezuelan. While Gálvez did not assume responsibility for this secret mission, when the time came to attack Jamaica, he would do very well to have up-to-date information about the island's defenses and its naval and military power. If someone had to be hanged for spying, he figured, better a Creole like Miranda than a Spaniard because of the repercussions executing a Spaniard could have.

In any case, it was already too late to turn back; Francisco de Miranda had already introduced himself to the English in Jamaica and begun negotiations with General Commander of the British Force John Dalling. The talks with the English general lasted more than four months, during which time Miranda traveled the length of Jamaica, taking notes on all the fortifications, castles, ports, defense batteries and estimating the number of military and naval troops.

Greasing a palm here and offering a bribe there, the Venezuelan additionally acquired very accurate maps of Jamaica, Kingston and Port Royal Bay.

After complex negotiations, Miranda also was successful in obtaining a written agreement with the English about the prisoner exchange. Cajigal, his immediate superior, approved the document as did Bernardo de Gálvez himself. To avoid problems, Gálvez then sought Madrid's approval. The agreement liberated a total of twenty-two officers and eight hundred and fifty soldiers, who boarded a schooner, two brigantines and two other British ships flying flags of truce bound for Cuba from Port Royal in December 1782. It was indisputable that the prisoner exchange was a success.

CHAPTER 43
Smuggling in Batanabó

To expedite the prisoner exchange, Francisco de Miranda had received a substantial advance from the treasury and, in addition, had secured a personal loan. On his return to Cuba, one of his problems was that he could not easily explain how he had spent the money he had budgeted for expenses. He could hardly confess to bribing English officials. But that was not the main problem Miranda faced when he returned from his mission. He returned to Cuba with a vessel loaded with English merchandise that Spanish customs absolutely prohibited from entering the island. After announcing the ship was going to land at the Cuban port of Trinidad, he ended up landing in the small port of Batanabó.

Miranda was unaware that the island intendant, Don Juan Ignacio Urriza, had had Miranda in his sights for some time, and the fact that Miranda had been absent from the island for no apparent reason had aroused Urriza's suspicions. The same day Miranda disembarked, believing he would more easily elude a search by customs in Batanabó, he was met by Urriza's men, who proceeded to seize Miranda's entire cargo. Among the purchases Miranda had made in Port Royal were several boxes containing books by Adam Smith, Lawrence Sterne (*Sentimental Journey*), John Milton and Tobías Smollet, but this was not the kind of contraband the intendant was interested in.

In an era when smuggling was rampant, an accepted part of Cuban life, it was not likely that a few bolts of cloth from Liverpool, a few barrels of whisky or a couple of sacks of flour would arouse the intendant's scrutiny. Urriza's was angling for bigger fish.

When the Captain General Cajigal found out that Miranda, his trusted aide, was being subjected to search and seizure of his belongings without so much as a by-your-leave, Cajigal ordered soldiers to arrest the customs agents Urriza had sent to the port. When Urriza would not budge, Cajigal tried to convince him to bury the case by telling him Miranda had gone to Jamaica on affairs of state, which only made the skeptical intendant more suspicious. Urriza, then, not only accused Miranda of attempting to profit from illegitimate commerce but also accused Cajigal of attempting to abuse his authority by silencing the whole shady business.

The fact was that Miranda's success in achieving the prisoner exchange as well as his fruitful labor as a spy was tainted by this incident, and after the quartermaster ordered his secretary to the Madrid court with documents detailing the accusations against the governor and his aide Miranda would face serious consequences.

When Cajigal found out the intendant had sent that communiqué to Madrid, he realized he should take the matter seriously and wrote to Secretary for the Indies José de Gálvez to dispel the accusations hanging over his aide's head once and for all. He also realized that at any moment these accusations could have repercussions for his own prestige. In the letter, Cajigal praised his aide to the heavens and revealed certain details–which he probably should have omitted—about the success of Miranda's espionage in Jamaica. Here was an intellectual from an excellent military background with the skills necessary to conduct difficult negotiations with the English. The governor praised Miranda to such an extent that, showing a terrible sense of timing, he requested a promotion for Francisco de Miranda. Cajigal wrote he was in Miranda's debt because of the success of his double mission to Jamaica.

Cajigal also wrote to Bernardo de Gálvez, perhaps thinking that he could intercede with his uncle on behalf of Miranda, next sent Miranda for a personal audience with Gálvez in Guarico. The first thing Colonel Miranda did was show Gálvez all the documents he had brought from Jamaica. He placed them neatly on the Gálvez's desk, and Gálvez read each one of the lists of ground troops and navy personnel and checked the maps of the island and the blue-prints of the fortifications, one by one.

"I see my friend Cajigal wasn't exaggerating when he informed me that you had gathered excellent information," Gálvez said, "although I assume you probably had to pay a very high price for these documents."

"Your Excellency knows very well that everything in life has its price. You and those who have enjoyed the immediate backing for your ambitions perhaps have not had to live through the embarrassment of having to beg, coerce and bribe to achieve your objectives. But those of us who can't count on a privileged background sometimes have to drag ourselves through the mud to get results."

Feeling something between surprise and annoyance, Gálvez stared at Miranda. "Señor Miranda, the truth is, I don't understand your reaction. I have just praised your work in Jamaica, and you answer me with a virtual insult."

"Forgive me, General, but I don't see how I've insulted you."

"From what you've just said, it could be inferred that those of us who were lucky to be born into a family of the lower nobility have had everything handed to us. I can assure you that has not been my case or that of any of my relatives. At one time, Cajigal himself commented that you belong to a well-off family in Caracas, probably one of greater means than the poor but titled noblemen in the Gálvez family. I assure you that many winters when the bacon preserved in lard and goat jerky ran out, as a child I had to stuff myself with prickly pears to assuage my hunger pangs."

Miranda seemed to understand this argument and relaxed his offensive.

Gálvez seized the moment to add, "Miranda, you may observe that I am speaking with complete candor. Believe me when I say I do so on behalf of our mutual friendship with Captain General Cajigal. You are a very intelligent man capable of doing a great service to his Majesty, but then you commit acts that detract from what you've achieved. I think that sometimes you are your own worst enemy!"

"Excellency, may I ask you to name these acts?"

"You already know what they are. Cajigal himself and I also know, although I have preferred to keep quiet out of respect for your friendship with the captain general." Gálvez pushed his chair back from his desk so he could open a drawer from which he removed a thick folder. "I don't need to open this dossier, but it contains no fewer than four warrants for your arrest."

"May I know what I'm accused of?"

Gálvez smiled. "Pardon me again for my bluntness, but perhaps it would be easier to tell you what you are *not* accused of. I hold here an old summary from the Inquisition about your possession of banned books, a letter from the Secretary for the Indies to Cajigal about the incident that arose from Campbell's visit to Havana, and finally a file from Customs concerning your attempt to bring in contraband goods from Jamaica."

"You know very well you can't accuse me of accompanying Campbell on his visit to the fortifications because I wasn't in Havana that day."

"The letter also mentions how your sympathies are with the English; although it's true you did not reveal them during General Campbell's recent visit, I had already noticed them during one of our conversations."

"I assure you, Excellency, that the fact that I admire British literature and culture does not mean I would not be willing to fight against England. I think I have sufficiently demonstrated that in the siege of Pensacola and by acquiring the information that could facilitate your taking Jamaica. As far as the accusation of acquiring banned books goes, with all due respect, it seems contradictory to me that a government calling itself enlightened, such as that of his Majesty Charles III, punishes us for reading the very authors responsible for the Enlightenment."

Gálvez could not respond because at that moment an orderly entered the office to announce that his wife was waiting for them on the terrace to have refreshments before lunch. Felicitas had met Miranda in Cuba and felt a certain affection for him. It was well known that Miranda was popular with the ladies, thanks to his eloquence and gallantry.

CHAPTER 44
The Attack on New Providence

As the head of Caribbean operations, Bernardo de Gálvez could not take direct action against Jamaica until the reinforcements arrived in Guarico, as had been stipulated with the French. That did not mean he could not take action when he saw that Caribbean waters were infested with corsairs of varying nationalities who did not respect flags or loyalties and practiced the philosophy, "It's always good fishing in troubled waters." He thus authorized Governor Cajigal to organize an attack from Cuba on the English island of New Providence, which had become the principal nest of corsairs devastating Caribbean waters by attacking not only mercantile ships but also small, solitary Spanish or French war ships.

When Cajigal tried to get the troop convoy to sail to the Bahamas protected by Spanish ships, he ran into strong resistance against ordering ships that were protecting Cuba to sail away, especially after the sails of Admiral Rodney's fleet were seen in the proximity of Havana. Once again, Captain General Cajigal put himself in Francisco de Miranda's hands. Miranda had a flotilla of brigantines from the English rebel colonies escort the troop convoy to New Providence. At the head of this flotilla was the American captain Alexander Gillon, the owner of the frigate The South Carolina.

Cajigal had imagined a risky, lightning strike on New Providence but worried that it could result in the English fleet patrolling in waters off Charlestown finding out about it and attacking the Spanish convoy from the rear. Regardless, Cajigal decided to go all in. The convoy ships and the American brigantines had barely arrived in Nassau, when

Cajigal sent his aide Miranda on the schooner Surprise with a letter addressed to the English governor, John Robert Maxwell. The letter was written as an ultimatum, assuring Maxwell that the Spanish fleet had surrounded the island and had blockaded the English fleet at Charlestown, which was a bluff suggested by Miranda. Cajigal wrote that if Maxwell did not yield immediately, the Spaniards would launch an attack against the island with uncommon force. He offered Maxwell twelve hours to surrender.

Francisco de Miranda's bluff paid off. Before the twelve hours were up, Governor Maxwell capitulated and began offering terms of surrender. He even thanked Cajigal for giving him time to think about his decision, "although that was the most difficult task I have ever undertaken as a soldier."

To prepare the written surrender, Miranda took special care to avoid the mistake made in the Pensacola surrender. Because no limits had been set on the English prisoners released from Pensacola, many of them went on to join the British army on other fronts in North America. This had even provoked the American Congress to lodge a protest with Madrid. The terms of surrender reached at New Providence, therefore, stipulated that any English prisoners freed were at no time to fight against any of England's enemies in the war.

As head of military operations in the Caribbean, Bernardo de Gálvez had somewhat reluctantly authorized the taking of New Providence, and even if the attack were successful, he thought the operation was small potatoes in comparison with his ambitious plan to attack Jamaica. However, once the attack on Nassau was concluded, Gálvez had to recognize the operation had been a success: the Spanish had captured twelve corsairs and sixty-five merchant marine ships. The impounded booty included numerous cannons, muskets and gunpowder. He, therefore, took pride in informing Madrid about it.

A while later, however, he received with a mix of surprise and consternation a communication from the Secretary for the Indies José de Gálvez that had a copy of a note from Secretary of the Navy Marquis González de Castejón attached. González de Castejón accused Captain General Cajigal of Cuba of an outrageous disregard for the King's instructions prohibiting direct cooperation with the Americans and underscored that Cajigal had acted with Bernardo de Gálvez's authorization. Furthermore, González de Castejón's communiqué included an order dated November 1781 stating, "It should never behoove us in aiding the war of the American colonists against their mother country with his Majesty's fleet and arms to create a bad example for rebellious spirits in our Indies. It would equally be very prejudicial for the King to become involved in the insurgent colonies' interests."

Thanks to his sense of discipline, Gálvez chose not to answer this communiqué as he might have wanted; he was aware the order was in flagrant contradiction to the instructions he'd been given by Secretary for the Indies' to help the rebel colonists with arms, munitions, supplies and large quantities of money. The original decision to help the Americans had been authorized at a cabinet meeting that González de Castejón himself had attended. The most surprising thing was that the order that Minister González de Castejón now brought up had been given two years after war had been declared on the English, tacitly or expressly, in alliance with the Americans.

Gálvez wondered if that tongue-lashing was González de Castejón's delayed revenge for the conflict with Captain Calvo de Irazábal and the other navy captains. Although at no time did he endorse González de Castejón's opinion, Gálvez honored his obligation to pass the Secretary of the Navy's note to Cajigal. Cajigal replied that González de Castejón's criticism was unjustified, because at no time had the American ships played a major role in the military conquest of New Providence; they had only escorted the Spanish convoy on a "Spanish and very Spanish" expedition.

At the end of his letter to the Secretary of the Navy, Cajigal included a note announcing that Miranda would visit Bernardo de Gálvez to discuss this and other matters.

CHAPTER 45
Mercury, God of Thieves

It was almost miraculous that orbiting in such a small galaxy Gálvez's and Miranda's stars had not yet suffered a head-on collision. The fact is both personalities were very powerful and resembled each other in certain respects: they were ambitious, outstanding leaders. Miranda's pride was based on his vast erudition and culture, while Gálvez's intelligence was oriented more toward problem-solving. As often happens, these two strong personalities clashed over a minor issue, the publication of an article in a Haitian newspaper about the taking of Nassau.

A little before Francisco de Miranda arrived on Guarico, the Governor Guillaume Leonard de Bellecombí of Haiti had given Gálvez a copy of an article published in *Affiches Americaines* that reported in detail on the Spanish expedition to the Bahamas and the conquest of Nassau. Although the article did not mention Miranda by name, it apparently indicated that he had been the brains behind the operation. What bothered Bernardo de Gálvez the most was that the news praised the Spanish negotiator of the English surrender in Nassau for avoiding the error made in Pensacola: allowing the defeated English troops to be reincorporated into the fight against the rebel colonies. Gálvez felt he had been indirectly blamed.

Gálvez had just received a copy of the newspaper, and it was still lying on his desk when Miranda entered his office. Miranda was so nervous, he did not notice the sour look on the general's face nor notice the newspaper. Almost before greeting Gálvez, Miranda launched his defense: "Your Excellency, it is my honor and duty to say to you that what we have here is a pack of lies that unerringly is conspiring to sully your actions and your honor, and ruin me. . . . " And Miranda proceeded to list the accusations weighing against him, which according to him were false. Then, not wanting to misstate anything, he read aloud a note he took out of his pocket: "With my record, and the authorities about to throw me in prison . . . bad luck and misfortune are pursuing me relentlessly. Without your extraordinary effort to protect me, I think my ruin is assured. However, I'll never fail to deliver what I promised, and I only beg you to swear on your honor that you'll tell me what tack I should I take (if I'm able) to control the damage to my honor and subsistence in the present circumstances."

Miranda looked around the room as if he were waiting for arresting officers to spring from the corners at any moment to arrest him. Despite Gálvez already being indignant at Miranda's indiscretion in having made public a Spanish military action in a French newspaper, when he saw that his visitor was in a frantic state, he attempted to control his anger by addressing Miranda in a relatively even tone.

"Señor Miranda, I am perfectly aware you are worried but, as I already said to you during our last conversation, I am convinced that either through carelessness or lack of prudence you yourself have caused this persecution. You should know that the only reason I myself have not carried out arrest warrants issued against you is due to the esteem in which I hold your superior, Don Juan Manuel Cajigal, who has blind faith in you and is willing to defend you through thick and thin."

Miranda's response was once again insolent. "Your Excellency may rest assured that if my governor defends me, it is because he has absolute faith in my performance."

Gálvez in turn adopted a harsher tone: "I would appreciate it, *Señor* Miranda, if you would avoid making me lose my temper, which I am maintaining with difficulty after receiving a French newspaper carrying the news of the taking of Nassau. It is written in such a way as to suggest you yourself are the author of the article."

Miranda, who had not even noticed the copy of *Affiches Americaines* on the desk, opted to deny Gálvez's charge: "I assure you, General, that I did not write that article."

"I don't care whether you wrote it or not, but it is evident that the one who did write it followed the testimony of a witness to those events to the letter, and that person can only be you. Besides, we all know you have a strong friendship with Mr. Roland, the publisher of the libel."

"I'm somewhat disappointed that a cultured man of your intelligence could consider my friendship with a bookseller a blot on my record. You yourself in prior conversations have confessed to me that you spent your free time on the island reading books unavailable in Spain."

Gálvez never imagined that Miranda, instead of apologizing for his indiscretion, was going to defend himself in that manner, but he understood it would be hard to make him see reason without calling his orderly to have him arrested.

"I don't want to waste any more time talking about the article, but I think you should know that, contrary to what the article says, the Bahamas expedition cannot be considered an operation of great importance. It was a minor battle in the total scheme of our operations."

That observation succeeded in profoundly wounding Miranda's pride. "Your Excellency, if you would take the time to consider the booty we collected in arms, vessels and captives, an operation you call minor, you'll doubtless have to admit that at least it has meant a substantial increase in army and navy stores."

Gálvez preferred to ignore the improper tone Miranda used in addressing his superior and made one last attempt to calm the visitor's nerves. "Miranda, I suppose you came to my office to ask for my help and, because I still consider you a gentleman, I ask you to give me your word of honor that you'll not repeat what I'm going to tell you."

Gálvez waited for Miranda to nod in affirmation before continuing. "Since I have your word, I'm warning you in total confidentiality that Don Juan Antonio de Uruñuela, magistrate of the Royal

Tribunal in Guatemala, is on his way to Havana to initiate an indictment for the alleged crime of smuggling, in which Cajigal is already implicated for an attempt at bribery. If I were you, I'd be more worried that the Secretary for the Indies, Don José de Gálvez y Gallardo, has knowledge of those accusations and will not rest until he sees you brought before a tribunal in Spain."

Miranda was taken aback and needed a few seconds to reply. "Your Excellency, if I understand you right, you are putting me on guard against the Secretary for the Indies, but isn't he a close family member of yours?"

"If what you're thinking is that I could intercede with my uncle on your behalf, it's because you do not know his character. Once Don José de Gálvez has made a decision, it's practically impossible to get him to change it. You may rest assured that if I were to dare to intercede on your behalf, the only thing I would achieve would be for him to include me on the list of suspects in this matter, which is exactly what just happened to Cajigal."

Miranda buried his chin in his chest as if had received a blow to the head. Gálvez took the opportunity to take out his watch so Miranda would understand that he had concluded the meeting. "With what I have just said to you, I think we have said everything we could say, and I would even go so far as to say we've said too much."

Like a fatally wounded bull who resists falling in the sand and keeps thrashing his horns around, Miranda had to attempt a last word. "If you'll permit me, Excellency, I have one last matter to address, though rest assured I won't keep you long."

"All right, but why don't we continue our conversation on the veranda. My legs tend to go to sleep if I spend too much time sitting in the same position . . . and I think my brain does too."

They walked out to the terrace facing the sea, and Gálvez asked the butler to bring two glasses of sherry.

Once he had taken a sip from his wine glass, Miranda seemed to calm down and speak in a normal tone of voice for the first time since the beginning of the conversation. "Please, Excellency, listen a few minutes more about a matter I believe of crucial importance. You already know how Urriza, the intendant, has an ax to grind with me and how he sent his bloodhounds to seize some merchandise. By transporting it, I was only returning, minimally, a big favor an English merchant had done me when he gave me secret information in person the last time I was in his office. In actuality, the merchandise was a bunch of inconsequential trifles. However, thanks to the scandal that has erupted, I have not dared follow up on what seems to be a much more important affair I'd like to bring to your Excellency's attention."

While the general sipped his sherry, Miranda explained that during his lengthy stay in Jamaica, he had met a merchant who had in his possession numerous containers of quicksilver that two English frigates had seized from a Spanish ship bound for South America. Since the British government had no direct use for the ore, the English navy had sold the cargo at a good price.

This time it was Gálvez who interrupted rather brusquely. "What do you propose doing with the quicksilver?"

"We are still in time, if we succeed in stopping Urriza's indictment and other outlandish accusations. . . . If we speak to the merchant and perhaps propose a deal, we could all benefit from it, above all the Spanish mining industry that needs the ore to finance the war with England."

Gálvez remained silent because he wanted to avoid a violent argument in his own house, but Miranda was so absorbed in his own speech, that he mistook Gálvez's silence for interest. Then, Miranda said the worst thing possible: "Besides, I understand that your uncle, Don José, among his many other responsibilities, has control over quicksilver production and transport. I thought perhaps if we were to interest him in the operation, then he could forget about some of the unfounded accusations made against my person."

At that very moment, the stars collided.

"Look, Miranda, up until now I have put up with arguments you've made that neither my military rank nor my honor can bear. But I'll say to you that your latest proposal is the straw that broke the camel's back. I would ask you, Miranda, not to say another word about this new act of smuggling you are proposing to me. The ore's unsavory origin can only dirty the hands of anyone who might want to be involved in that scheme."

Gálvez's tone was so dry and blunt that for once Miranda was speechless.

"Before the butler escorts you to the door," Gálvez continued, "I only want to say to you that a few years ago, I had the occasion to visit a quicksilver mine, and the experience left me with a very bad taste in my mouth. Now you, unawares, have gone and mentioned the noose in the hanged man's house. To conclude, given that you always try to dazzle others with your erudition, I'll tell you I too am familiar with the names of the Greek and Roman gods, and I remind you that Mercury—which is the same name as quicksilver—was the patron of thieves."

It would be the last time Gálvez would ever see Miranda, because on his return to Cuba, Miranda decided to leave for the United States on the American sloop Prudent, with letters of recommendation for General Washington and other congressional leaders with whom Juan Manuel Cajigal had corresponded previously.

Unfortunately, the serious charges against Francisco de Miranda had also damaged Juan Manuel Cajigal's reputation; in short order, he was replaced and sent back to Spain and prosecuted for smuggling and bribery. The painful duty of slapping shackles on one of the most brilliant soldiers born in Cuba and then throwing him in jail fell to Bernardo's uncle, Antonio de Gálvez, the bay commander.

Shortly after Cajigal's dismissal and arrest, sails appeared on Guarico's horizon that everyone believed was an advanced squadron of Admiral Comte de Grasse's fleet. Unfortunately, the Marquis of Vaudreil, the squad commander, landed and told Gálvez that his ships were only a remnant of the French fleet that was supposed to support the Spaniards in the taking of Jamaica. On approaching the island of Dominique, Admiral Rodney's fleet caught up to the French fleet, because Admiral Grasse had made the mistake of waiting for the transport convoy. Rodney succeeded in breaking the combat line, decimating the French ships and taking Admiral Grasse prisoner.

The Marquis of Vaudreil cried when he related the magnitude of the naval disaster, in which the French had lost five ships of the line and three thousand men, among them their best captains. Gálvez was most upset when he realized that, after this defeat, another French fleet would never be sent to join his own in launching the attack on Jamaica.

In any case, Gálvez would not have the honor of leading the joint operation. Shortly thereafter, he received a secret dispatch in which the Secretary for the Indies José de Gálvez announced that His Majesty King Charles III and the Christian King Louis XVI had jointly decided to relieve him of his command of the army and the armada in the Jamaican campaign. They had appointed to replace him a French naval officer, Admiral d'Estaing, whose fleet was already en route to the Antilles.

It was small consolation to Gálvez that his removal and the Frenchman's appointment as head of Caribbean operations were not fulfilled. At the beginning of 1783, an armistice was declared, thus interrupting any military action, including the projected Jamaican campaign.

Part Six

CHAPTER 46
The End of John Jay's Mission to Spain

Mr. And Mrs. Jay's troubles in Madrid were smoothed over when Sarah gave birth to a little girl, which was a source of great joy and satisfaction for the baby's parents. Their euphoria at the baby's birth was reported in letters to their family members, which ridiculed the Papist environment they were living in and joked about good Hortensia's recommendations to her mistress, such as baptizing the baby immediately with the name of the saint corresponding to that date. In that regard, the baby's father commented in a letter to his father-in-law, "The Spaniards are very proud to count on a saint for every day of the year, but since the saints are at war with the heretics like us, it would be better if we named her for some sinner, who will probably appreciate it more."

When poor Hortensia tried to explain to them in her broken English that they should baptize the child right away to avoid having her end up in Limbo if she died, her comment made the new mother laugh. She explained in a letter to a friend the Catholic Church's notion of a place between Heaven and Hell, "a dark refuge inhabited by the souls of children who died unbaptized."

Unfortunately, her laughter turned into sorrow when the servant's dark predictions came true: the newborn girl began to suffer convulsions, which in a few days ended her fragile existence. The tragedy made Sarah Livingston even sadder and, from what the few Spaniards who frequented their house could observe, her mood probably had a detrimental effect on her husband's progress in completing the mission the American Congress had entrusted to him.

Secretary of State Floridablanca again made use of Diego María Gardoqui from Bilbao, who had previously served as interpreter when Commissioner Arthur Lee journeyed to Spain. In an attempt to elude direct contact with Jay, he had Gardoqui mollify Jay with vague promises. When Gardoqui visited them in their house on San Mateo Street, he had the occasion to observe the relationship between the American and his wife up close and was surprised how much Sarah Livingston dominated her husband John.

Before they began their trip to Europe, Sarah's father, with his Puritan mentality, had warned his daughter against the decadent and sumptuous European courts and recommended to her that she not "fall into joys and worldly pleasures and, above all, the so-called 'high life,' which will drive from your mind your habitual common sense and piety." William Livingston could not imagine that during her stay in Madrid his daughter would remain unacquainted with the excesses of a decadent society because, in fact, she was living in a social vacuum.

The American envoy had arrived in Spain with the principal mission of establishing a friendly reciprocal trade agreement similar to the one the rebel colonies had succeeded in signing with France. When John Jay was finally received by Floridablanca, the Secretary of State declared that the treaty that the American Congress was proposing could not include the same clauses as the French pact because the interests of each country, although united by Bourbon monarchies, were completely different. Floridablanca was convinced that he could put off the American delegate indefinitely with vague promises and use Gardoqui's good offices to placate the emissary. Accordingly, he sent a secret note to his ministry secretary that read,

Dear Sir and dear friend:

In responding to Jay, it's better Gardoqui accompany him and tell him we won't stop aiding him, as long as we have the means to do so. . . . We shall do what is possible to aid the colonies in providing uniforms and other goods. Ultimately, to broaden the King's instructions, it is necessary to show signs of effective reciprocity in establishing a solid friendship and confidence without resorting to words and protests with the usual polite phrases. Gardoqui should sound out those men with that and see what he can get out of them.

As to the military and financial aid that the Spanish government had promised on several occasions to the representatives of the American Congress, the circumstances had changed. Upon declaring war on England, Spain had to deal with overspending while at the same time the treasury was suffering from the lack of funds being generated by her American colonies, due to the insecurity of maritime traffic. Without completely denying responsibility for the aid, Floridablanca was dodging Jay about how and when it would be carried out.

Jay faced yet another difficult problem: the urgency of securing funds to fight the war with England. Before he had left for Spain, the American Congress had drawn bills of exchange in the amount of one hundred thousand pounds sterling in his name. However, the congress had done so without consulting with the Spanish government and without negotiating the conditions of the operation. Perhaps the congress was confident that, based on Spain's earlier promises of subsidy, the Crown would endorse the bills of exchange upon the arrival of their envoy in Madrid or at least concede enough credit to him to cash them when they matured, which was soon.

But not having been consulted previously, the Spanish government absolutely refused to endorse them, and Floridablanca limited himself to offering certain subsidies at a much lower rate to the congressional representative. During the two years he was in Spain, the sword of Damocles of those bills of exchange hung over John Jay's head and negatively influenced his ability to carry out his mission.

Perhaps the most delicate mission, however, that Congress assigned to Jay was to convince Spain to recognize the United States' right of navigation on the Mississippi. Both nations considered this to be an inalienable right and, for the American rebels, the southern states access to the Gulf of Mexico for shipping their goods was indispensible to their economy. The problem of the right of navigation on the great river had already led to conflict between the two governments; long before Jay's arrival in Spain, Spain's unofficial representative in Philadelphia, Juan de Miralles, had warned José de Gálvez about Congress' inflexibility on this point.

For his part, Secretary of State Floridablanca's tortuous mind was convinced that the best thing for Spain would be for the war to linger on and weaken England as well as the rebel colonies. Then, the two Bourbon monarchies would be the lords and masters of land and sea. This hypothesis was not realistic because when two countries are at war, one usually wins; and at that time it seemed that the United States was winning the war. From the Spanish embassy in Paris, the Count of Aranda kept predicting that it could be dangerous not to court the good will of the victor, even before a definitive victory. However, since the ambassador did not get along with the Secretary of State and had fallen out of the King's favor, no one heeded his advice at Court.

The covert way in which a large part of Spanish aid to the rebels had been carried out had provoked the distrust of such important political figures as James Madison, who declared his complete opposition to John Jay's recognizing the exclusion Spain wished to impose. "I have always considered Spain's mysterious and reserved behavior, particularly its negligence in money matters," he had said, "to be designed to force us to submit. Spain has shown a mighty indifference to our cause rather than any alliance with us."

None other than Benjamin Franklin himself also backed Jay's insistence on the rights of navigation on the Mississippi. In his correspondence from Paris to Jay, Franklin had recommended absolute firmness: "I'd prefer to buy all Spanish rights on the Mississippi River at a high price before selling one drop of its waters." The way the Spanish government had treated the representative of his country also angered Franklin: "If Spain has taken four years to decide if its government should negotiate with us or not, give it forty more and meanwhile we'll mind our own business."

Ultimately, Franklin requested Jay go to Paris to help him with the peace negotiations. Jay thanked his lucky stars and, as soon as he received the opportune congressional authorization, packed his bags and left Madrid. Yet, Jay had not secured an agreement concerning the right of way on the Mississippi. And he had not even been officially recognized by the Spanish government as his country's ambassador. Thus, he left Madrid resentful and angry. On crossing the border in the Pyrenees, Jay probably shook the dust from his shoes, happy to be free of Spanish soil, and his wife Sarah Livingston probably did the same, even more vigorously.

CHAPTER 47
St. Maxent in Paris

Although Gilbert Antoine de St. Maxent's grandfather and father were modest lower noblemen from Longwy, a small village in Lorraine, his grandfather, Joseph Dupré, changed his original surname to the more sonorous St. Maxent. When the young Gilbert emigrated to French Louisiana to dedicate himself to the fur trade with the Indians in the upper Mississippi and the slave trade for the southern plantations, he could never have imagined that, through his daughters' marriages, he would become related to Spanish nobility and that his grandchildren would have the titles of counts and barons. His eldest daughter, Isabel, married Lieutenant General Luis de Unzaga; Felicitas married Bernardo de Gálvez; Mariana married Colonel Manuel Flon y Quesada, the Count of La Cadena; María Josefa married Lieutenant Colonel Joaquín Osorno; and María Mercedes married Capitan Louis Ferriet y Pichón, Baron of Ferriet.

The gossip was that in order to marry off his daughters to illustrious Spanish officers, Gilbert Antoine had had to overlook those amorous officers' initial dalliances with his beautiful daughters that had taken place under his own roof. But, in the end, they all ended up married and with happy families. As the proverb goes, "All's well that ends well."

Precisely a little after the armistice between Spain and England was signed in the middle of 1783, St. Maxent was visiting the French capital to negotiate some commercial deals on behalf of the Spanish government, thanks to his son-in-law Bernardo de Gálvez's recommendation. Gálvez had maintained his position as governor of Louisiana and the two Floridas even while residing in Guarico and had communicated to Madrid his concern about the Indians that had arisen during the Pensacola campaign: most of the tribes in the region had made alliances with England, with dire consequences for the Spanish troops.

The ups and downs of the last war seemed to have made the bureaucrats more dim-witted in understanding the need to attract a majority of the population in North America, whose territories could be a barrier to the predictable spread of masses of European settlers thirsting for land in the West, and no less savage and aggressive than the Indians.

Following his son-in-law's suggestion, before going to Paris St. Maxent stopped in Madrid to receive his commission as a commercial agent for Spain in trading with all the Indian nations in the territory recently won from England. His trip to France, then, was for visiting businesses that would provide the merchandise to be sold to the Indians.

Around the same time, the representatives of England, Spain, France and the United States began arriving in Paris to negotiate a peace treaty. Establishing the borders across North America for the post-war was one of the treaty's most important objectives. The Spanish government had again entrusted the Count of Aranda with negotiating the peace agreements. Bernardo de Gálvez had recommended his father-in-law, St. Maxent, to Aranda, detailing St. Maxent's experiences as a trapper and trader traveling the entire upper Mississippi and its tributaries. Aranda understood immediately that almost by accident he had a true expert on the great river at his disposal. One of the objectives of the peace negotiations with the Americans was precisely the issue of the Mississippi.

In pursuit of negotiating the peace treaties, the American Congress had reinforced its delegation in Paris with two new delegates: one was John Jay, still smarting from the treatment he had received in Madrid, and the other was John Adams, a Boston lawyer who had the reputation of being uncompromising and stubborn. The latter perhaps was chosen precisely to counterbalance the Spanish Ambassador Aranda's stubbornness at the negotiating table.

Even before beginning the talks, Aranda had experienced an involuntary disagreement with John Jay, who despite being the youngest member of the delegation had the loudest voice. Apparently, Jay had arrived at the Spanish embassy without prior notice and, when he was not able to meet with Aranda, left there angry. Then, when the Spanish ambassador wanted to visit Jay, the American diplomat replied he was not available.

Apart from frictions that were mere issues of protocol, each party came to the table with such contrary assumptions that it was impossible to arrive at an agreement. Jay alleged that in defeating England, the United States subrogated the rights of the British Empire over that territory, while the Spaniards maintained that all territories Bernardo de Gálvez had won in his campaigns against the English belonged to Spain by right of conquest.

In one of the first meetings about boundaries in Ambassador Aranda's office, Aranda unrolled a large map of North America, which included the entire Mississippi River, from its source to its mouth in New Orleans. With pencil in hand, the ambassador drew a borderline above the confluence of the Missouri and the Ohio Rivers and showed it to the American diplomats. John Jay immediately asked Aranda for the same pencil with which he had marked the map and drew a new borderline from the river's source almost to the river's mouth. Jay's reasoning reflected the borders of the new southern states as reaching to the eastern bank of the mighty Mississippi.

In the dispatch Aranda sent to Madrid informing the government about the interview, he protested, "Mister Jay is determined to make the entire Mississippi River the border. It may be deduced that either he has no talent, or that he came with no instructions other than to use the name Mississippi, or that he's arguing in bad faith." Next, he mentioned the boundaries that, in responding to Jay's much broader interpretation, he had proposed to his opponent, "I went to the tip of the Great Lakes specifically. Then I moved down the map to the confluence of the Great Conhaway and the Ohio Rivers to look for the closest bend in South Carolina to continue the border visually to a lake in the Appalachian Mountains."

At that time, Gilbert Antoine de St. Maxent was a guest in Aranda's house, and Aranda showed his guest the borders Spain was proposing after the stormy meeting with John Jay. The former fur trapper confirmed that indeed those were the territorial boundaries that he knew from traveling there during his time trading with the Indians.

Always exhausted after negotiating with the Americans, Aranda retired with St. Maxent to the library, where a good fire was stoked, and Aranda invited his guest to a glass of fine French cognac. He winked at St. Maxent (with his one good eye, since the other was permanently clouded) and commented, "Dear St. Maxent, you and I are farmers, and we know that when the planting season is over, if the seeds are sown late and they grow, there'll be few crops to harvest."

St. Maxent did not understand what Aranda's metaphor had to do with the negotiations. In reality, Aranda, a landowner of vast holdings, was referring to the lost opportunity to sow friendship with the new nation's representatives. Once the rebel colonists had won the battle with the mother country, they were not keen on making major concessions to Spain, whose attitude had been ambiguous, to say the least, and sometimes contradictory.

CHAPTER 48
Mrs. Jay Loses Her Temper

Despite his reputation for being stubborn and uncompromising, Ambassador Aranda knew how to sacrifice his pride and offer an olive branch to the other side in his negotiations with the American delegation. As it was an open secret that in the Jays' marriage, Sarah Livingston wore the pants, Aranda invited Jay and his wife to a luncheon at his home "in the French style", which meant it did not follow Spanish protocol. Now, a luncheon in the Spanish Embassy was nothing to sneeze at, given that Aranda had one of the best chefs and the most exquisite wines in Paris. Aranda had set an elegant table, trusting that the delights offered would make John and Sarah forget the unpleasantness they had experienced in Spain.

At the table, Aranda seated Gilbert Antoine de St. Maxent to the left of Sarah, who assumed that the Creole was of French nationality given his fluency. An old fox, St. Maxent had barely spoken a few words with Sarah, when he realized that behind her apparently gentle, fresh face and the clarity of those blue eyes was a strong woman. Sarah inserted into the conversation some revolutionary concepts that usually were well received in her sophisticated French social milieu, but which St. Maxent did not appreciate. One did not talk of politics in polite company, especially not with women.

"It may surprise you to know that some ladies of the higher echelons of French aristocracy," said Sarah on seeing her table mate was not responding to her, "have accepted the progressive ideas we've brought from the other side of the Atlantic."

"Mrs. Jay, I'm sure those posh ladies are very interested in those ideas, which you know how to articulate so convincingly, but if I were you, I would ask those noble ladies if they would be willing to apply those liberal ideas to their own extensive properties, where an owner can hang a poacher for killing a deer on his hunting grounds."

By the way he talked, Sarah understood that St. Maxent was not completely French and even suspected he was a Spaniard in disguise. The host had seated him at her side to see what she thought of him; once she associated her dinner companion with Spain, Mrs. Jay began a rabid diatribe against the country where she had lived for the last few years.

The food the waiters were serving was exquisite, and the wine had an extraordinary bouquet. St. Maxent, not enjoying the conversation, made the most of sampling the delicacies served while trying to ignore the slings and arrows against Spain that sprang from that lady's sweet lips. As Sarah recalled those unpleasant memories, she lost some of her angelic expression, and her white cheeks reddened with anger. Assuming her tablemate was very interested in what she was saying, she described in detail about her trip from Cádiz that had forced her to travel through a poor and dusty region.

"Near a place called Ciudad Real, one of the muleteers who had frequented the mines told me mercury ore, needed to amalgamate silver in Mexico, is still being extracted. He told me all the men who work there are convicts who have committed serious crimes. And once they are imprisoned there, they never see daylight again. Each day, they are led through an underground passage from the dungeons to the mine's well. Doesn't it seem to you that this way of treating those condemned men indicates the Spaniards' lack of feeling towards their own citizens, even if the latter are criminals?"

Sarah interpreted his silence as tacit agreement, so she went on to criticize the political system and, above all, the colonial system that the Spaniards had used in the Americas. According to Mrs. Jay, this contrasted with the Anglo-Saxon's benevolent and humanitarian attitude towards colonization, that is, their pioneers had gone to America only seeking fertile lands to work and had not enslaved the natives nor had they an obsession with finding gold and silver.

At this point, St. Maxent was tired of listening to Sarah's chatter or perhaps he had drunk too much wine, because he answered, "My lady, I have lived for many years in a French colony that later became Spanish and I sincerely think the Spanish system of colonization is no better or worse than that of other European countries. Neither do I think their treatment of the Indians is worse than the English and the French winning them over by getting them drunk on firewater. What I can tell you is that if you are proud of how the New England colonists have treated the natives, you should ask any member of the several northern tribes about it who were kicked off their lands, saw their villages swept away and had their populations decimated.

Although a lady of liberal ideas should be able to tolerate differences of opinion, Sarah Livinsgston resented those comments and, during the rest of the meal, spoke not another word to her table mate. When the banquet was over, she arose from her chair without saying goodbye to St. Maxent.

Later, when St. Maxent and Ambassador Aranda were alone in the library, drinking coffee and a glass of cognac, Aranda informed his guest that he had not missed a moment of his verbal jousting with Mrs. Jay. "I think you've done very well in stopping her in her tracks, that harpy with her nun-like airs. It's clear the Americans are still too boorish to act civilized. What poppycock to spout at an embassy dinner? Couldn't she guess that I, her host, was listening to all that nonsense?"

"It's obvious the woman was mouthing all the prejudices the English have inculcated in her from childhood, although the Americans are fighting against the English now. Besides, I think the blame for that arrogant attitude falls not just to the Americans, but also on the French, who are buttering them up and waiting to benefit from their newfound independence."

Aranda nodded his head in agreement while he was snorting a pinch of snuff. He completely agreed with St. Maxent that the French had placed the leaders of the American independence movement on a pedestal, thereby encouraging their arrogance.

Precisely in those days at the Academy of Sciences an homage to the philosopher Voltaire was being celebrated at an event where Benjamin Franklin was also present. Since the diplomatic corps was invited, the Count of Aranda took Gilbert Antoine with him, reasoning that it would be a great opportunity for his friend to witness such a spectacle, typical of the Age of Enlightenment.

A Spanish aristocrat's mentor who was also present at the Academy's homage described the meeting between the two great men as follows:

The famous philosopher Benjamin Franklin, the liberator of English America, his homeland, was there. He went over to receive Voltaire and the two embraced and kissed each other's cheeks to more applause from the audience.

Voltaire, old, thin, wrinkled, an octogenarian, was wearing an old-fashioned black velvet waistcoat, a pink dress shirt with silver designs on it to the knees, knee-high stockings and boots, and lace ruffles at the end of the shirtsleeves almost to his fingertips. A tie, but with three knots, and his crutch. Franklin wore a long, tan waistcoat, with stockings of the same color, a large tie, his own salt and pepper hair slicked behind his ears, which didn't quite reach to his shoulder, a very erudite, bald pate and his spectacles. He was a man of about seventy, a mite stout, with ruddy cheeks.

CHAPTER 49
The Porcelain Vase

After the banquet Ambassador Aranda had given for John Jay and his wife, he realized that in the two crucial matters of negotiation— the navigation rights on the Mississippi and the northern border of Louisiana—it would be impossible to come to an agreement with John Jay, who was the dominant voice in the delegation. Jay was so confident he had the support of Congress on the issue that he did not even bother listening to the other party's arguments. Aranda hoped that, because of his age as well as his character, he might find a more reasonable ear in the chief of the American delegation, who was still nominally Dr. Franklin. Aranda took advantage of one of John Jay's trips out of Paris to visit Franklin. Ambassador Aranda had barely begun discussing the issue, when he realized that Dr. Franklin's position was just as uncompromising.

"I wonder if it's worth selling my front door to a powerful enemy," Franklin said to him, cutting off any possibility of dialogue.

In his tireless battle to defend the rights acquired by Spain in North America, Aranda did not have a leg to stand on, not only because of the Americans' obstinacy, but because of lack of support from the Spanish government. Neither did he obtain the firm backing of the French Minister, who should have been the Spanish Ambassador's principal ally.

Although apparently the Count of Vergennes agreed with Aranda, he criticized him behind his back for his pride and stubbornness: "I've negotiated with the Turks, and that says everything. . . . Even so, I've never seen anything like this ambassador."

It was true that Aranda's prideful character and his lack of compromise concerning issues of protocol had not earned him friends at Louis XVI's court. Surely the great ladies and the powdered-wig fops who frequented the halls of Versailles would have preferred dealing with a courtly gentleman who didn't defend his country's interests with such tenacity. In one of her letters, the famous Madame d'Epinay confessed that she had been very disappointed when there appeared in Versailles "a stooped man, of sallow complexion, hard of hearing (except when he was being praised), cross-eyed, toothless and with his nose congested with snuff, who in the halls usually had nothing to say and when he did speak, it was to be rude."

Despite his physical appearance and his somewhat clumsy manners, the Count of Aranda had a superior intelligence that allowed him to anticipate events and, just as he had predicted what the Americans' attitude would be once they won the war, he guessed that the two principal enemies in the war would be drawn together rather than drawn to their allies.

While Gilbert Antoine de St. Maxent was living at the embassy, the Count of Aranda used him as his confidant and, when he returned home after negotiating with the Americans for hours without achieving a positive result, he would escort his guest to the library and, after opening a bottle of cognac, would share his disappointments and frustrations with him.

"My dear St. Maxent, if anyone believes that after this war the English and the Americans will never be friends again, they are absolutely mistaken. The fact is that even after four years of the cruelest of wars, the Anglo-Saxons on both sides of the Atlantic still have many interests in common. I've been saying for some time that they are going to come to an understanding behind France's and Spain's backs and then they will slam the door in our faces."

Aranda's hunches were often based on the information he had been collecting over the years, thanks to his informers in all the principal European capitals. Aranda put his glass of cognac and his box of snuff on the table for a moment, then hunted among the perfectly numbered folders in his archive and finally found what he was looking for: a letter that Benjamín Franklin had addressed to the

British Prime Minster, Lord Howe, when he realized it was going to be very hard to achieve a peaceful accord between the colonies and the English Parliament. Aranda read aloud Franklin's letter that had already been translated from English to French: "For a long time, I made the effort with sincere, indefatigable zeal to prevent this fine and noble porcelain vase that is the British empire from shattering because I knew that, once it was broken, the pieces could not retain the value and strength they had as a whole. One could hardly expect those pieces to go back together again."

"As you can appreciate," Aranda went on, "these statements are not those of someone who has decided on a complete break. It means that, despite appearances, the revolutionary leaders somehow keep hoping to repair their relationship with the motherland."

Yet for all his foresight, Aranda could not imagine that while he was conversing with St. Maxent, John Jay had just arrived in London. He had traveled there without informing the rest of the delegation to reach a separate peace with England. The proposal that Jay took to London did not even have Congress' approval. It assumed the immediate recognition and total independence of the thirteen colonies, yielding the right of navigation on the Mississippi to all new states and recognizing the great river's left bank as the new country's western border.

The offer was highly tempting for the British, given that it was based on their historic rights to a territory they no longer possessed. While they seemed to behave generously towards their colonies, they were actually sowing the seeds of discord between the new United States and Spain, thereby taking revenge on the Spaniards for their contribution to the American victory.

When Jay returned to Paris with the agreement in hand, his fellow delegates had no choice but to congratulate him, although they understood that his behavior was tantamount to disloyalty to old Benjamin Franklin and the rest of the delegates. Franklin, who had welcomed John Jay and his wife as if they were family members, putting them up in his house in Passy when they arrived in France, felt especially hurt by this disloyal gesture but did not have the strength or the desire to revoke the agreement in any way. Although late, it did glue back together the pieces of the porcelain vase to which he had alluded in his letter to Lord Howe.

As the actual head of the American delegation, Franklin had the thankless job of communicating the news to the Count of Vergennes, who screamed bloody murder and accused the Americans of being ungrateful for the important aid that the colonists had received from France. Plus, they were breaking a treaty previously signed in 1778 between the two countries, which obligated the United States and France to act in tandem in any action that might suppose coming to an understanding with the enemy.

Franklin's answer to Vergennes' outburst demonstrated the American's fine diplomatic sense. On the one hand, he assured him that the treaty with England would not be definitive until France had weighed in, and on the other hand, he pointed out that their ally's outrage was precisely what the English were expecting. According to Franklin, the British were boasting they had succeeded in dividing them. Thus, if no one paid much attention to the misunderstanding, it would be the British themselves who would feel disappointed.

When the Count of Aranda found out about the Americans' treachery, he also screamed bloody murder, but they were the screams of a diplomat undermined by his own government and steadily deceived by his allies. His was a voice crying in the wilderness. His deadly predictions were coming true. He noted that the Madrid government was ignoring his recommendations to establish a binding agreement with the congressional representatives:

This federal republic was born a pigmy, in a manner of speaking, and it has needed the support and strength of two powerful states like Spain and France to achieve independence. The day will come when it will grow and become a giant and a fearsome colossus in those regions. Then it will forget the benefits it received from the two powers and only think about its own agrandissement.

Given the fait accompli, Aranda and the Duke of Manchester had no choice but to sign the peace treaty between Spain and Great

Britain on September 3, 1783, the same date that the American delegates, Franklin, Adams and Jay, signed with the Englishman David Hartley the peace treaty between the United States and Great Britain.

Although Ambassador Aranda had not been completely satisfied with the terms of the agreement, which included nothing concrete about the border or the thorny issue of navigation on the Mississippi, he did recognize that, under the circumstances, more had been obtained than what had been expected.

CHAPTER 50
The Egg Shell

(Felicitas de St. Maxent speaks)

In the convent of the "Petites Seurs du Sacré Coeur" (The Little Sisters of the Sacred Heart) in New Orleans, the nuns made us memorize whole paragraphs of *The Conquest of Gaul*. Although with the passing years I've forgotten almost everything except the beginning "Galia est omni divisa in partes . . . ," those stanzas evoked very vivid scenes in my youthful imagination. With great realism I imagined Julius Caesar entering Rome on a chariot drawn by lively, white steeds, escorted by centurions carrying gleaming lances and shields, while being hailed by the multitude throwing rose petals as the conquering general went by.

Those images from my childhood came to mind when Bernardo and I journeyed to the capital so that my husband could receive from the King himself the titles and honors he had earned during the war with England, especially the taking of Pensacola, which had become renown in all of Spain as the most brilliant victory of the entire war.

During our stop in Havana, Bernardo had received dispatches naming him the Count of Gálvez. Due to issues of protocol, he had first been awarded the Viscounty of Galvezton (later Galveston). I realized what that meant even more after arriving in Madrid, when we received a color drawing of the coat of arms, which included images that already appeared on the Gálvez family crest, but perhaps the most significant image that was added to the crest was a small brigantine ship representing the Galvezton. The motto read, "I alone," the phrase my husband had spoken before sailing in front of the Red Cliffs batteries. It now became the motto for the title of nobility conferred on him by the King.

In the first days after our arrival in the capital, where we were housed in a magnificent mansion near the Buenavista Palace and the picturesque Cibeles fountain, we allowed ourselves to become intoxicated by the sweet wine of fame and adulation. The first time someone addressed me as Countess, I felt I had at last scaled the social ladder. The ladies of Havana, who touted their ancient Spanish pedigree, had resisted treating me—a Creole, brown-skinned widow—as a social equal on numerous occasions. After the multitude of receptions had ended, a few days had to pass for the dust to settle and for our egos to return to normal. But as Spanish high society was highly frivolous, soon another novelty cropped up to distract its members from wining and dining the hero of Pensacola and his Creole wife. When Bernardo and I were alone in that immense palace, we looked at ourselves in the mirror and realized that, with or without a royal title, we were still the same people.

In that regard, let me emphasize that although Bernardo readily accepted the gestures of appreciation and warmth of the government, the aristocracy and the common people, he wanted to be kept informed about how the negotiations were progressing in Paris. Perhaps he intuited that the politicians and diplomats could lose with a pen stroke what he had won with the sword. In addition to the dispatches sent by Ambassador Aranda to his Uncle José, Bernardo had a source of unofficial and privileged information in the letters that my father sent him from Paris, where he was serving as advisor on the border issue.

Thanks to that information, Bernardo understood much better than those who were receiving Aranda's dispatches what was involved in defining the borders of the upper Mississippi. Since the news he was receiving from Paris were not very reassuring, I noticed that Bernardo was becoming increasingly nervous, to the point that he stopped accompanying me on my strolls through the parks and avenues of Spain's capital, where members of the aristocracy mixed with the commoners and shared their games and pastimes. Bernardo had been given a position in the palace with the fancy title of Supervisor of Veteran Soldiers in the Americas, but with very little to do. He was somewhat busy reviewing the reports and maps that successive Louisiana governors and intendants had sent to the government. With these, my husband could claim Spain's historic rights to those territories.

Bernardo was so absorbed in his work on his own self-imposed schedule that when he returned home late, he did not want to have dinner and went to bed immediately without wanting to speak to anyone, not even to me. But being that we slept in the same room, I noticed that Bernardo returned home in such a state of agitation that he could not go to sleep.

One night, I don't know if he was still dreaming or in a state of restless sleep, I heard him exclaim, "The King himself is to blame for what's happening because he's as stubborn as a mule and nobody can make him change his mind. From the beginning of this war, he decided not to recognize the American insurgents and, now that the war is over, he won't be strong-armed, even though it could cost him half of his American dominions!"

Even if it was a dream, that outburst worried me. I had heard terrible things about the punishments inflicted on people who showed a lack of respect or insulted the person of the King. I had even been told that during the time the Count of Aranda was president of the Council of Castile, a man who had hurled insults against the King had had his tongue torn out. I had heard it said in Madrid that, "So that the Holy Inquisition does not find out about some things, you mustn't even think them."

As a very special favor, his Uncle José proposed Bernardo accompany him to a luncheon that his Majesty was holding in a palace dining room, an event to which only leading figures were invited, high ranking officials in the government as well as ambassadors and Spanish grandees. That afternoon, I waited at home for my husband because I was very curious about how the royal luncheon had transpired. I was even more intrigued to know how he had reacted in the palace setting that he had had no interest in frequenting as of late. Doubtless it was a rare experience to see a king behind closed doors.

Instead of returning happy and pleased with what he had witnessed, Bernardo came home swearing. Up until then I had never heard him express himself so harshly, not only about the court but about the King himself. As soon as Bernardo stepped down from the carriage that brought him back, I noticed he looked upset. He prudently said nothing in front of the servants, but he gestured for me to join him upstairs in a small room next to our bedroom so we could talk alone. Once he shut the dressing room door, Bernardo took off his jacket, which he threw on the floor, along with the belt holding his sword, and gave free rein to his indignation.

"I assure you, my dear Felicitas, I've never attended a more absurd and less edifying performance. It doesn't speak well of those who organize the court's activities that a group of government ministers, who should have other more urgent things to do, can waste an entire morning watching our sovereign eat. Among those present were European ambassadors and an assortment of Spanish grandees, who are great in title only. The chamberlains who have the honor of attending to his needs all have fancy titles, but they often make mistakes and trip over each other in their eagerness to be the first to serve his Majesty."

I tried to calm him by taking one of his hands in mine and patting his cheeks, which was a gesture of mine he liked, but Bernardo continued describing what he had witnessed in highly critical terms.

"The only suspense-filled moment was when the King cracked the shell of a hard-boiled egg with a small spoon. Then a sepulchral silence spread throughout the room to see if his Majesty hit the middle of the egg just right with his little silver spoon. Once the King has consumed the shell's content, the shell must maintain its delicate balance in the small silver egg cup. If, as it appears that this is almost always the case, the King achieves this ingenuous juggling act, the chamberlain removes the plate immediately before the spoon or the egg can fall, and all the gathered courtiers applaud."

Afraid that he'd do something foolish if I left him alone in such a nervous state, I asked Bernardo to accompany me on my usual stroll around the city at that hour. We drove down in the carriage to a small chapel built on the shore of the Manzanares River and rode up via a road that runs parallel to the river, where some fishermen were trying their luck by throwing a hook into the clear waters flowing down from the sierra.

When we arrived at the Toledo Bridge, we leaned over the stone parapet to enjoy the view afforded by the Manzanares, which meandered placidly as it flowed down from its springs in the Guadarrama Sierra. At that hour, the mountains emerged from behind some hills covered in stands of oaks, turning shades of red and blue. This was exactly the area of El Pardo, where the King liked to hunt. The sun was setting over the treetops and vegetation of the riverbank.

After contemplating the landscape in silence for a while, Bernardo put his arms around my waist and said, "Felicitas, you'll doubtless have noticed the great beauty of the landscape, but it does not have the power or pull of what we who have lived on the other side of the sea have seen. This river may serve as inspiration to painters in Madrid, but it lacks force and drama. You know that the least of the Mississippi's tributaries is mightier than the Manzanares. Although the Father of Waters has occasionally given me a thrashing, I feel happier on its river banks than almost anywhere.

CHAPTER 51

Dinner at the Minister for the Indies' Home

(Felicitas St. Maxent speaks)

That evening, the two of us went to dine at Uncle José's and his wife Doña María Concepción Valenzuela de Fuentes' home. She is Don José's third wife, a marriage that had allowed him to associate with the oldest Castilian aristocracy and, what's more, to receive a substantial dowry from her father, the Count of Puebla. Doña María Concepción is thirty years younger than her husband, so we are more or less the same age. Yet, despite our intimate family ties, there is no love lost between us.

Beforehand, I'd suspected that, despite my new title of countess, Don José's wife would not think that a Creole woman from New Orleans, ennobled only by her husband's merits and a noble Castilian family, could have the same upper-class standing. Since these sentiments usually are mutual, I thought María Concepción was lacking a bit in feminine charm. Well, I didn't like the way she curled her upper lip, making her moustache hairs bunch up, as if she were a grenadier corporal, when she thought she was saying something important.

That night, Doña María Concepción shined as an excellent hostess. She had prepared a high-class army of liveried servants, who offered the guests varied dishes arranged on Sevres porcelain plates, each more delectable than the last, and poured different varieties of wine into Murano crystal flutes whose stems were so fine that in lifting the glasses one was in danger of breaking them. The Spanish Ambassador to France, the Marquis of Ossun, Don Pedro Rodríguez de Campomanes and the French advisor to the Treasury Secretary, Pierre de Cabarrús, who was organizing a financial mechanism called Royal IOUs (*vales reales*) on assignment for the King, attended the dinner. Cabarrús was also busy with the creation of the San Carlos Bank to deal with the large expenses incurred during the recent war, many of which originated with the financial aid and the supplies administered at the behest of the United States Congress.

Cabarrús, seated by my side, enjoyed my company and spoke to me in perfect French, perhaps a bit different from what I had learned in Louisiana, but he said he found my accent charming. Everything went smoothly during the dinner, and the quality of the dishes as well as the bouquet of the wines was commented on favorably by all, including the French ambassador who, with scant diplomatic tact, on occasion complained that Spanish cuisine was a bit rudimentary in comparison to the gastronomical sophistication to be found north of the Pyrenees.

Before having dessert served, Don José arose from his chair and, after offering the traditional toast to the King of Spain's health and additionally to the French King's health–in deference to the French ambassador's presence—indicated that he had very important news to tell those assembled.

"Today, the news that the various interested parties have finally signed the Treaty of Paris has been received by special delivery at court. I have the pleasure to announce that His Majesty has done very well in the treaty. The English have ceded to us the entire Mississippi basin, the two Floridas, including the towns of Mobile, Pensacola and St. Augustine, so we can pride ourselves on having secured the major Spanish objective of this war, which was to the throw the English out of the Gulf of Mexico."

Perhaps Don José was hoping his statement would provoke the applause of those gathered, or at least a murmur of approval, but the women, as was usual in these cases, remained silent and, in contrast, several of the gentlemen asked questions that the minister was surely not expecting.

"What finally happened concerning Gibraltar? I thought its return was perhaps the main objective of entering the war," asked Don Pedro Rodríguez de Campomanes.

Don José glanced knowingly at the guest to his right, the French ambassador. His country had pledged in its treaty with Spain not to sign the peace until the English had returned Gibraltar; but the Marquis of Ossun seemed too busy spooning his mandarin sorbet to participate in the conversation.

"In the end, it has not been possible to secure Gibraltar's return to us, but on the other hand, we've recovered the island of Menorca, which was under British rule all this time," Uncle José ended up admitting after a pregnant pause.

"Has the repayment of financial and military aid we've lent to the new country these last few years been arranged with the Americans?" asked Cabarrús, in turn.

After Uncle José's second pregnant pause, he answered, "It would behoove whoever is aware of the different sums and provisions sent to the Americans to provide the amount of what our allies owe us to the treasury, even if it's a rough estimate."

Probably feeling supported by those who had asked the earlier questions, Bernardo asked, "Is it known if the United States congressional representatives have accepted the terms of Spain's exclusive right of navigation on the Mississippi River and the establishment of the border at the river's head?"

I noticed that our host, who had already answered the other guests' questions unwillingly, was livid that his own nephew would put him on the spot by raising an issue for which Uncle José did not have a satisfactory response.

"The United States delegates did not want any accord on the question of borders," his uncle replied a bit abruptly to Bernardo, "but if you wish, we'll have the opportunity to discuss this issue in greater detail without having to bore the ladies and the other guests concerning a matter that is surely of no interest to them."

As soon as the last guest had left, I saw Uncle José gesture to Bernardo for him to accompany him to an adjoining room, whose door he promptly shut. María Concepción and I remained in the salon trying to make awkward conversation, but meanwhile we were each anxious to hear what was happening in the next room. Although it was obvious Uncle José had called his nephew to account for what he considered an indiscretion, Bernardo was not willing to accept a rebuke for it. Through the door we could hear some of their conversation quickly become heated and boil over into an argument. What surprised me was that, while eavesdropping, I realized that the one who was speaking more forcefully and in a higher pitch of voice was not the minister but my husband.

Perhaps as a result of the argument Bernardo and his uncle had the night of the dinner, Don José decided not to show him the text of the treaties that had arrived from Paris, but my father did send Bernardo a detailed report about the results of the negotiations. In the treaty signed in Versailles by the Count of Aranda and the Duke of Manchester, the English King ceded the two Floridas to the Spanish Crown without specifying their borders. However, in the previous agreement that John Jay had negotiated in London, England, a line had been drawn between the Mississippi and Apalachicola Rivers, which passed through the 31st parallel, and fixed the southern border of its domains there (preserving entirely the Canadian territory). According to Aranda's calculations, Spain's dominions reached much further north, to the 35th parallel. Moreover, in the eighth article of the treaty signed by the United States and England, free navigation on the Mississippi for the English was established. The borderline that had been drawn in the earlier accord subtracted the part of the territory Bernardo had taken from the English from Spanish dominion, except Natchez, and placed Spanish Louisiana's southern border barely ten leagues as the crow flies on the Gulf of Mexico.

After learning these details, thanks to my father, Bernardo sought an audience with the King to to tell him that the terms of the agreement with the American Congress were illegal, because both banks of the Mississippi had been under Spanish control before the negotiations had started and that, overriding any other precedent, the recent right of conquest could not be ignored. But Uncle José would not authorize such a meeting, fearing that my husband would be too explicit in his presentation to the King. I too understood that it could be dangerous for anyone to make the King see that the peace he was so proud of had not met some of his principal objectives and could be a motive for conflict with the new American state.

For a time, Bernardo was left to busy himself with supervising the troops in Spanish America, but the unfolding of events soon made the King understand that Bernardo was the only person capable of defending the rights of Spain in the region. Therefore, the King reconfirmed Bernardo's earlier appointment as governor of Louisiana and the two Floridas. In addition, he was named capitán general of Cuba, where he could organize, if necessary, the defense of the Spanish territories in North America.

I had the impression that this time, Don José had not used his influence to further his nephew's career. Rather, this new appointment was a way for Don José to rid the Court of someone who had a very critical opinion of the way the government was proceeding with respect to the United States and who was willing to defend his point of view, come hell or high water.

CHAPTER 52
Gardoqui is Named Ambassador

The Count of Floridablanca had not anticipated the dangers inherent in treating the congressional delegates in a cavalier manner, when he received the news in 1784 that John Jay would probably be appointed the new nation's secretary of state. He immediately went to Diego Gardoqui for his opinion on that possible appointment. The Basque merchant replied bluntly that if Jay were confirmed, he would try to do Spain as much harm as possible.

Even before the news became known, Floridablanca had thought about the possibility of sending Gardoqui as the Spanish ambassador to the new United States, because the merchant had developed a friendship with John Jay himself and his wife during the time they were in Madrid. Gardoqui, who had lived temporarily in London as a consul and the official in charge of war reparations, had resisted traveling to America, alleging that, after the death of his mother, Simona de Arriquibar, he had to deal with pressing family business. The appointment of John Jay as secretary of state, on the one hand, led the Spanish government to press the Americans to accept an ambassador, and perhaps even Gardoqui himself understood that he was the best person to carry out the difficult mission.

Once Gardoqui accepted the appointment as *chargé d'affaires* to the American congress, Floridablanca requested he give him his impressions of Secretary of State Jay and his wife. Gardoqui, who was usually very discreet and reticent, replied expansively:

Jay, the American who is generally considered very talented and capable of hiding his known weakness, for the most part, shows that he is not a disinterested party and that his wife accentuates that passion because, beyond her high self-esteem and extreme vanity, she likes people to give her gifts and even more that they regale her. The woman, whom he loves blindly, dominates him, and he does nothing without her consent to such an extent that her opinion prevails, even if her husband initially disagrees. I infer from this that with a little finesse in dealing with her and a few well-timed dinners, you'll secure the friendship of each. . . .

He is not the only one in his country who has the same weakness, because there are many more in government service. I think anyone adept at seizing the moment by entertaining them and, above all, plying them with good wine, will achieve the desired result without giving the game away.

Floridablanca took his ambassador's report so literally that he immediately requested new funds for "entertainment and gifts" for the American politicians and their families. Floridablanca gave Gardoqui some very concrete instructions for his arrival in Philadelphia: to negotiate a treaty between Spain and the United States establishing the borders of their respective territories and denying the new republic the right of navigation on the Mississippi. In exchange for this transfer, Spain would offer the new state the economic privileges of most favored nation status.

Floridablanca asked Gardoqui to stay in constant contact with Captain General Bernardo de Gálvez in Havana because of the latter's extensive experience in North America. Indeed, when Gardoqui stopped over in Havana, before leaving for Philadelphia he awaited Bernardo de Gálvez's arrival from Spain. To assure the perfect coordination between Gálvez and Gardoqui, Floridablanca had given each an identical kit of codes so they could correspond secretly with each other.

Gálvez had already demonstrated his contentious character on various occasions and he recommended to Gardoqui not to let the Americans intimidate him. The Americans had shown they had inherited in large part their former colonial masters' arrogance and in no small measure their hypocrisy. Characteristically vehement, Gálvez suggested to Gardoqui that he remind the American government about Spain's role in the fight for independence as soon as he had a chance by pointing out that the only rights the Americans had with respect to the Mississippi were rights of gratitude and not of usurpation. "If they were to speak unreasonably in threatening terms, you must disdain them, Sir, with the understanding that we aren't afraid of them. In the area, we have massive veteran troops, an auxiliary, seasoned militia and the friendship of many Indian nations, who have deserted the Americans and have enough guerrilla war experience in the forest. The Americans may think this tactic is exclusively theirs, but it is not."

Gardoqui listened closely to everything Gálvez said, without replying, although he might have answered that he had been appointed the Spanish envoy to the United States to better Spain's relationship with that country, not to declare war on them. Seated in front of Gálvez's desk, Gardoqui mused to himself about the trip they had taken together when Gálvez had just been appointed colonel of the Louisiana Standing Regiment; the tables had turned. In the past, Gardoqui was the teacher and mentor, and now it was Gálvez who was giving him advice. Although the business Gardoqui ran had sent ships to five continents, he had never embarked on a crossing longer than going from the Bay of Biscay to the southern English coast.

Indeed, Gardoqui's clothing was incompatible with Cuba's tropical climate. His dark suit made of heavy cloth, the same one he wore in Bilbao to go to the port stores, made him sweat profusely. When he went out, he put on a wide-brimmed straw hat to protect him from the tropical sun. The contrast between his black suit and his white hat was so pronounced that he looked like a strange bird, a penguin washed up on the beaches of Cuba by a rogue current.

Gardoqui's difficulty adapting to his environment went beyond his inadequate attire. As soon as he embarked from Cádiz, Gardoqui realized he had been wrong to accept the mission Floridablanca had entrusted to him; his absence from Bilbao could spell the ruin and even the bankruptcy of "Gardoqui and Sons," a company his father and grandfather had nurtured with such care. But the Basque had a strong sense of loyalty to the King and felt obligated to accept the mission.

CHAPTER 53
Oliver Pollock's Debts

Gálvez and Gardoqui were still immersed in studying the maps of the Louisiana territory and the land north of the Floridas, when an aide passed a note to Captain General Gálvez. After reading the message, Gálvez put away the dispatches they had been perusing and rolled up the maps they had been consulting.

Then, he said to Gardoqui, "Forgive me, my friend, but I have to attend to an urgent matter. If you're willing, we can pick this up in my office this afternoon and continue working."

The carriage waiting at the door of the General Captaincy took Gálvez to La Cabaña prison, where Judge Sebastián Larrañaga awaited him. Gálvez had already arranged to have Oliver Pollock, who had been locked up there for more than a year for not paying his creditors, released.

"I've brought the amount of bail you told to me and, if you'll allow me, I'll take the prisoner with me right now."

"If that's what you want, I'll sign the order releasing Mr. Pollock immediately," the judge replied.

The man who emerged from the prison dungeon a while later only looked remotely like the Oliver Pollock Bernardo de Gálvez had known in New Orleans, when he had joined him on his ship in the company of Governor Unzaga. If he had passed him in the street, Gálvez probably would not have recognized the American congress' former agent.

In a nutshell, Pollock's troubles had begun when Gálvez was no longer in Louisiana during his campaigns in the Gulf of Mexico. The

219

Irishman's generosity coupled with his carelessness had, over time, been the downfall of one of the most prosperous landowners and merchants in the whole region. Oliver Pollock was not alone in making the mistake of trying to secure the necessary funding for the new United States to survive, but he had not concerned himself with accurate bookkeeping. More from a lack of professionalism than from a desire to commit fraud, he had not clearly separated his personal finances from the congress' treasury, in this case the Virginia General Assembly's treasury.

In the last years of the war, the Continental Army's expenses had been so exorbitant that the ability to get funds to Oliver Pollock as well as to others who were striving to achieve the same result, including merchant Robert Morris, considered by many to be the financier of the American Revolution, had been exceeded by quite a bit. Pollock's lack of accurate bookkeeping had resulted in his mixing his own debts with the debts he accumulated in the name of the new administration to the point that it was impossible to untangle them. As a consequence of several failed real estate deals in Louisiana, Pollock had lost his plantations and, when he tried to avoid bankruptcy by asking the governor of Virginia to reimburse him some of the funds he had been anticipating, the state administrators replied that they could hardly help him when Congress itself was bankrupt.

In a last-ditch effort to straighten out his financial situation, Pollock had traveled to Havana, where he had business dealings with Spanish entrepreneurs who were part of the so-called Floridean clan, the same men who had been involved in the molasses and slave trade between Florida ports and the island de Cuba. But this last desperate effort to secure funds turned against Pollock, when the same people he had approached for credit demanded the return of significant amounts of money lent in past ventures. Pollock could not pay and was thrown into jail.

After posting Pollock's bail with his own money, Bernardo de Gálvez took him to his home on the coast, hoping the ocean air and sunlight would be therapeutic for someone who had spent more than a year in a dark, dank dungeon.

On arriving at his residence, Gálvez explained, "I've given instructions to the butler to give you whatever you need, including a change of clothes and, if you like, refreshments. You may stay in our home for as long as you like. My house is your house because Spain cannot forget everything you did to help us in the war against the English."

Pollock willingly accepted the hospitality the captain general offered him and took Gálvez's hand between his hands to contain the emotion he felt at having been rescued by his former co-conspirator.

A little while later, Gálvez's aide informed him that his guest had requested to see him. Gálvez was greeted by a freshly bathed and clean-shaven man, more like the Oliver Pollock he had known in New Orleans. But with his sunken cheeks, formerly so plump, and his forehead's deep wrinkles, he had lost his baby face; the intense pallor of his face seemed to have erased even the sprinkle of freckles that had been the Irishman's most characteristic feature. His formerly red sideburns were now a premature mix of salt and pepper.

Oliver Pollock noticed, too, that the years that had passed had worn on Gálvez as well. Some things did not change, however; even when he was speaking about very serious matters, Gálvez spoke with a twinkle in his dark eyes and a sardonic smile. Behind that smile, nevertheless, Pollock thought he detected bitterness. Pollock had witnessed Gálvez's abdominal injury in Pensacola and he remembered that the scar had not healed properly. Yet something made the Irishman guess that Bernardo de Gálvez carried deeper scars inside.

Without saying a word, each preferred not to mention painful memories but to celebrate instead the fact that they were still alive. Many of those who had fought for the same cause had ended up at the bottom of the ocean or had been blasted into bits as the English garrison at Half Moon Fort had been. Although each wanted to wipe a wet cloth over the blackboard of his memory, some events that they had lived together came to the surface, almost inevitably.

"General, I want to beg your forgiveness, because I wasn't able to express my profound gratitude this morning when you came to get me out of jail and paid the bail the judge had imposed to satisfy my creditors."

"I've already told you that you don't have to thank me. All of us who participated in the taking of Pensacola are indebted to you. I am especially grateful because, if I hadn't had the information you gave me about the Red Cliffs battery, perhaps I wouldn't have dared enter the port, and everything would have turned out differently."

"The only thing I am grateful for is that while I was locked up in prison is that I had time to think. I can assure you that on many occasions, I remembered the moment you decided to embark on the Galvezton and cross in front of the English cannon fire."

"It's true that at the time I was willing to gamble everything, but without a doubt what you me told after visiting the Red Cliffs helped me make my decision."

"Yes, but something I've only understood in remembering that incredible adventure is that you, General, could not have been one hundred percent sure the English cannon fire would not reach you."

Gálvez recovered the smile that Pollock had seen playing about his face. "Well, the fact is that one of those projectiles split the foremast rigging in two, piercing the canvas just inches from the mast itself. If that cannonball had hit the mast, I wouldn't be here now, and Spain probably wouldn't have retaken Pensacola."

"That's exactly what I thought. Although I believed you could sail through the channel untouched by the rain of fire from the English batteries, you only had one way of proving it: get aboard the Galvezton and set your course."

And so went their reminiscences as they sat out on the terrace facing the port dock, bathed in the setting sun's reddish reflections. The view looked very much like it had that afternoon when Gálvez had sailed past the Red Cliffs' barrage that had lit up the surface of the Pensacola Bay waters. Seeing that the light was dimming, Gálvez remembered he had made an appointment for that very afternoon to meet with Diego Gardoqui in his office.

"I would gladly stay here chatting with you, but I have an appointment in my office with the Spanish ambassador to Philadelphia, who is currently in Havana. Have you heard of Diego Gardo-qui?"

"I recognize that name. I seem to remember he was one of the people busily acquiring arms and provisions in Spain to be sent on to New Orleans?"

"Indeed, Gardoqui played an important role in sending aid. In fact, he acted as a Spanish government agent, just as you did for the American Congress, but from the other side of the Atlantic. If you don't mind, I would like him to meet you."

Once the captain general introduced them to each other in his office, Gardoqui and Pollock bonded immediately. Thanks to Spain's secrecy in sending aid to the United States, neither key player had ever met the other in arranging for the shipment of arms, medicine, clothing and other supplies to the army fighting in the upper Mississippi River.

In a twist of fate, three people who had contributed decisively to the victory of the United States army over England had come together purely by accident in Havana.

CHAPTER 54
The Halberdier's Diary

While Bernardo de Gálvez was still in route to Havana, on stopping over at the island of Puerto Rico, he received the sad news that his father, Matías, had just died in Mexico. Gálvez had only been in Cuba for fewer than five months, when he received a dispatch asking him to travel to New Spain to occupy the post of viceroy that his father had held.

The little time that they had spent in Cuba, Bernardo and Felicitas had been the center of attention and were hugely popular, but the reception awaiting them in May 1785, when they arrived in Mexico truly reached a climax. The fact that Bernardo was the son of a viceroy, who had left efficiency and honesty in government in his wake, contributed to his popularity, so much so that the King had waved Gálvez's mandatory inspection. The people appreciated above all that the new Viceroy Bernardo de Gálvez had served in New Spain years before, when he had first arrived in Mexico accompanying his uncle, Inspector General José de Gálvez. Back then, the young officer had spread a wave of warmth and congeniality in many places in the viceroyalty. Nevertheless, the opinion persisted in some quarters that Gálvez had sometimes acted in a reckless and irresponsible way, as in when he had risked the lives of his soldiers unnecessarily in battle with the Apaches; this was perhaps the only thing clouding his reputation.

In the streets of the capital this couplet was sung:

Yo te conocí pepita	I knew you
antes que fueras melón.	When you were only a seed.
	Now you've grown to a melon,

| *Maneja bien el bastón* | use you cane of command wisely. |
| *y cuida a la francesita.* | And take care of the French lady. |

Given that he was the King's supreme representative, the viceroy assumed the powers of the monarch himself. A very elaborate process unfolded in a series of steps from the moment Gálvez disembarked at the port of Veracruz to assume his post. Upon his arrival there, the new viceroy stopped at the same places and symbolically retraced the steps taken by Hernán Cortés, who had conquered the Aztec Empire for the Spanish Crown.

The new viceroy did not receive the command staff symbolizing his authority until he reached San Cristóbal Ecatepec. He made another important stop along the way at the Guadalupe Cathedral, accompanied by his family and the numerous members of his entourage; there, the priests received them beneath a canopy. The entire retinue attended a solemn Mass celebrating the promise of the viceroy's long and fruitful rule. After attending a solemn "Te Deum," Bernardo and Felicitas could finally head to the viceregal palace in the capital, where the most spectacular reception awaited them. The viceregal retinue filed past the troops, who presented arms and fired salvos of welcome. The multitude that had spread rose petals along the parade route and erected arches of triumph to celebrate the occasion, cheered for them as the viceroy passed by.

Their arrival at what would be their official residence did not mean the end of the festivities. A series of banquets and parties ensued that were paid for by the Town Hall and the Mexican Consulate. The special joy and expectation that attended this viceroy's arrival had made the cost of the receptions rise to the exorbitant amount of thirty thousand *pesos*. When these numbers reached Madrid, the King himself was scandalized by how much had been spent and he ordered that, from then on, the amount that could be lavished on such events should be limited to five thousand *pesos*. Thus, Viceroy Bernardo de Gálvez's reception was the last one to be celebrated with such splendor.

Bernardo de Gálvez had barely taken over, when he became aware that the situation in the viceroyalty was not very promising.

As if the Father of Waters had wanted to thrash the new viceroy by chasing the clouds from the sky, a lengthy drought had scorched part of the harvest in the past few months, and the little that remained had burned before it could be harvested by a series of killer frosts unfrequent in this warm climate. Famine ensued. The lack of wheat and corn had two equally negative effects: the first was that when their crops failed the farmers abandoned their lands and hit the road to the capital, where they hoped to find some sort of aid. The second and worst effect was a cruel epidemic of plague, which decimated the population throughout the viceroyalty.

The new viceroy, who had known how to fight against adversity at other times in his life, adopted drastic measures to stop the plague and the famine. To combat the epidemic, Gálvez decreed a public notice that absolute isolation of the sick was required to avoid contagion. He additionally established a system of confinement and free medication in the hospitals for the poor. To alleviate the effects of hunger, he called for an emergency meeting of the richest people in the viceroyalty, where he pressed them to make large donations. To set an example, the viceroy himself contributed sixteen thousand *pesos* of his own savings to the emergency fund and succeeded in convincing the richest families to loan him some one hundred thousand *pesos.*

To shelter the indigent masses flooding the capital's streets, at least temporarily, Gálvez gave instructions to the convents to house that army of emaciated men, women and children, who looked like walking cadavers. In addition, to set an example, he opened the viceregal palace doors to them.

There were serious deficiencies in agriculture policy unrelated to the hard freezes and bad harvests that had helped to deepen the famine: the obligatory banking of seeds had given rise to certain abuses. Some unscrupulous merchants benefitted from the shortages by hiking the price of the wheat and the corn they hoarded. When Viceroy Gálvez found out what was happening, he himself went to the nearest granary exchange and, with the help of two constables, chased out the crooked dealers with whips, just as Jesus Christ had done when he drove the moneychangers from the temple.

The initial admiration Viceroy Gálvez had inspired in the poor had become adoration, especially when they saw he enjoyed their entertainments and being among them. Palace halberdier José Gómez's wrote in his diary that, of all the viceroys he had known, Gálvez was the best because of his concern for the less fortunate as well as his love of merrymaking. The latter was recorded by Gómez: "In Mexico City on November 14, 1785 the first bullfight took place in the Plaza del Volador, and the viceroy and his wife circled the bullring in their carriage in the morning and afternoon. At night, there was a tower of colorful fireworks, the best I'd ever seen, and afterwards on a stage set up for the musicians, there was a typical dance. With the viceroy present, the viceroy's wife the countess was the first one on the dance floor, and then the other ladies followed suit, something that over time no one would believe, but that's the way it was."

Perhaps what contributed most to the respect and admiration with which the lower classes regarded the new viceroy of Mexico was his humanitarian gestures. The halberdier José Gómez reported in his diary on one of them: "In Mexico City on April 8, 1786 there was great news in the kingdom. On leaving the Acordada jail, men judged and condemned to death were on their way to the gallows. By a stroke of luck, Viceroy and Count of Gálvez was riding his horse, Pensil Americano and, having come across the prisoners, he pardoned them in the name of our Lord the King. The people began to shout, 'Long live Viceroy Gálvez!'"

Some mean-spirited citizens saw in that pardon a sure sign that Bernardo de Gálvez had ulterior motives for which he was trying to win over the people's confidence and support. The same naysayers cast doubt about whether Gálvez's meeting with the prisoners had been sheer coincidence or whether it had been staged, given that the Acordada court was obligated to notify the viceroy of the exact date and time executions were to take place. According to the halberdier's account and as the viceroy himself explained in his dispatch to the Minister for the Indies José de Gálvez, it was a coincidence.

In any case, when Don José de Gálvez, a stickler for jurisprudence with a tremendous respect for the law, read about the incident, he sent a letter to his nephew with a stern reprimand, stating that only the King had the right to issue pardons and, therefore, by pardoning the life of those prisoners, Bernardo de Gálvez had acted irregularly. What irked the minister about his nephew's gesture was not so much that he had usurped the monarch's exclusive prerogative, but that his nephew's conduct might provoke criticism from those who resented the Gálvez family wielding excessive power. This fear had already inspired a rhyme that circulated in Mexico when Bernardo's father was still alive:

> *¿Quién manda en este mundo?*   Who rules the Earth?
> *José, el primero.*   José, the first.
> *Matías, el segundo,*   Matías, the second,
> *y Bernardo, el tercero.*   and Bernardo, the third.
>
> *Fiscal . . . Virrey,*   Prosecutor . . . Viceroy,
> *Virrey . . . Ministro,*   Viceroy . . . Minister,
> *y Ministro . . . Rey.*   and Minister . . . King.
>
> *El Padre, aquí,*   Here, the Father,
> *El Hijo en La Habana,*   in Havana, the Son,
> *y el Espíritu en España.*   and in Spain, the Holy Ghost.

Indeed, the same people who had criticized the concentration of power in the hands of the Gálvez family, also mocked the drastic measures Bernardo had taken to control the famine and the epidemic. They saw his actions as a way of winning the people's love by any means so they would support him in breaking ties with Spain and declaring himself sovereign in that territory. According to this far-fetched argument, granting a pardon was part of a perfectly calculated plan to gain absolute power in the New Spain viceroyalty. Since the letter that José de Gálvez sent to his nephew had passed through several hands, some individuals used the reprimand to spread the rumor that the nephew had fallen from grace with his powerful uncle; it was but a small leap from that opinion to the declaration that Gálvez had lost the King's confidence.

The most curious thing about the life of these lies was that the more absurd they were, the more widespread they became. The resulting scandals imitated the effect a stone thrown into a pond has, with the rings created by the impact rippling all the way to the shore. From the moment that the rumor that Bernardo de Gálvez intended to mount a coup d'état spread, any new project undertaken by the viceroy was interpreted in that context.

Indeed, that happened with the renovations of the Chapultepec Castle, which, nevertheless, had already been planned by several of his predecessors and had even obtained the approval of the Ministry for the Indies under Viceroy Matías de Gálvez. In Pre-Colombian times, this high point overseeing the whole Tenochtitlán Valley was used as a resting place by the Aztec emperors, including Moctezuma II. In the colonial era, a palace was built there that had lodged illustrious guests, but after an ammunition dump explosion, part of the building had fallen into disrepair. The new viceroy thought that, in replacing the venerable building, he had found the right spot to move the new viceregal palace. Also, it would not be in the middle of the city center, where the viceroy's every move triggered a public procession.

Gálvez enthusiastically dedicated himself to reviewing the blueprints that the Colonel of Engineers Francisco Bambitelli had already presented to his father, introducing personal details such as relocating the bedrooms of the viceroy and the viceroy's wife to the same place, which was not how they were laid out in the viceregal palace on the central plaza. But what contributed to stoking the rumors about the viceroy's true designs was that the military engineer had fortified Chapultepec Castle with moats and high walls, which was not extraordinary if one thought about the building being the residence of the supreme authority in New Spain. Nevertheless, an avalanche of gossip followed the viceroy's request to construct underground passages so he could leave or enter the place without having to use the steep path leading to the top of the promontory.

CHAPTER 55
Collusion at the Inquisition

The bells had already rung at midnight in the cathedral tower when a freezing draft blew through the streets of Mexico City. The cold was the perfect pretext for men to wrap themselves in their capes, hide their faces in the cape folds, pull their wide-brimmed hats down to their eyebrows and make their way from different points of the city to the Palace of the Inquisition.

A little after midnight, the seven hooded men who had agreed to meet in the Inquisition's headquarters arrived at the back door of the building that, judging by the creaking of its rusty hinges, had rarely been opened. The names of those who participated in that conclave are not known, but the branch of government where they serve is. They entered the inner-most room and sat down around a table presided over by a cleric who did not remove his hood the entire time the meeting lasted.

A Holy Office magistrate addressed the group: "As you well know, we are gathered here to analyze a serious situation that has arisen in the viceroyalty, thanks to the nefarious designs of a man who at present occupies the highest office in New Spain. Our King's confidence and benevolence gave him the power he wields and that he now wishes to usurp. God save the King."

A Royal Audience Judge followed: "I think we have already spent too much time at other meetings analyzing the motives for this leader's behavior, a man who prefers to associate himself with the commoners rather than with those of us who have attained a position of authority by the Monarch's grace. I would venture to add that he-who-shall-not-be-named is infected with the same revolutionary ideas that led the English colonies to declare their independence from their mother country. Well, we know that he corresponded with the revolutionary leaders who now are in power in the new republic while he was governor of Louisiana."

Next, an Acordada court judge added his sentiments: "I would like to reiterate that we shouldn't waste any more time analyzing the situation but instead take action. It looks as if the maximum authority who should be enforcing the laws is the man who goes out of his way to disobey them. This is the first time we have gathered since his outrageous act of granting a pardon to prisoners on their way to the gallows. He had neither the power nor the authority to do so. Therefore, I would like to underscore for our brothers gathered here that his behavior not only establishes a grim precedent for keeping order but has also done irreparable harm to the court's prestige. After considering all the material and legal evidence of the case, we must decide on his sentence."

A Michoacán landowner also spoke: "As has already been said here, I think more speeches are unnecessary, when the time for action is now. Every day new irregularities are being committed that stoke feelings of rebellion in the lower classes. If we do not attack the problem soon, the totality of our colony, which our ancestors worked so hard to build with their sweat and blood, will be undone. If wheat and corn are being distributed by the bucketful from the granaries at laughable prices, who's going to sow the fields and maintain the crops, when no workers are left willing to put their backs into it?"

A mine proprietor from Guanajuato spoke on his interests: "The question that our brother has asked about the future of agriculture may be applied to other sectors that constitute the fundamental pillars of our economy and the viceroyalty's well-being. Where are we going to find miners who will risk descending into deep shafts if they are paid better in any other fresh-air job that the present administration has created in the name of remedying the famine and giving work to idle hands?"

A military engineer then addressed the group: "I too am just as concerned as our brother who has just spoken and want to express my own fear when I see large sums of money being earmarked for the fortification of Chapultepec Castle. I wonder why a viceregal palace needs high walls and deep moats, which, according to military strategy, are intended to repel an enemy attack. But from whom would the tenant who occupies that bastion must defend himself, if not from his own ambition? As a military engineer, I have no qualms about publicizing that this Castle is not being built as a residence but as a military fort able to repel an attack or, in this case, to launch an attack from that stronghold. I am perfectly happy to proclaim what is already an open secret. It would be impossible to keep secret the construction of a building where more than four thousand people—men, boys and all sorts of craftsmen—are already working."

Lastly, one of the clerics at the cathedral spoke: "Just as our brother who has just spoken about the construction of Chapultepec Castle has said, I too am fully aware and can speak knowledgeably about the sums it's costing to restore the two cathedral towers affected by the earthquake a few years ago. It is strange that someone who worries so much about the cathedral's façade should visit the temple's interior so infrequently. As the rhyme circulating throughout the city says, this individual is devoted to attending bullfights, dances and parties, but is very seldom seen attending church and prayers:

En todas partes te veo,	I see you everywhere,
excepto en el jubileo.	except at Holy Mass.

The seven men gathered there were conscious that what was being proposed and planned was a serious crime. If what had been said around that table got to the ears of he-who-shall-not be-named, some of them would end up thrown in jail, if not swinging from the gallows. Perhaps their awareness of their own precariousness was what drove them to make a snap decision. After styling themselves members of a star chamber, one and all of the conspirators agreed to put an end to the pretensions of the viceroy, which could only be resolved with his death or removal. Then, one of the hooded men, who was also an apothecary, proposed the surest and most discrete way to proceed to achieve their aims.

Meanwhile, completely oblivious to this plot, Bernardo de Gálvez and his wife Felicitas had gone on an outing at San Augustín de las Cuevas. During one of their strolls, people crowded around them, which upset the guards who accompanied them. The couple's short vacation was hardly restful, as the halberdier José Gómez wrote in his diary, "More than a relaxing vacation, it was a blur: two days of bullfights, cock fights, fandangos and games, even dog fights, in all the plazas and streets for all the social classes. Since the time of the Conquest, no one had ever seen anything like it in this kingdom. No viceroy had ever been so applauded and hailed as the Count of Gálvez was."

CHAPTER 56
The Viceroy's Confession
(Felicitas de St. Maxent speaks)

On our return from visiting San Augustín de las Cuevas, Bernardo suffered a wave of nausea, vomiting and diarrhea that made me fear for his life. At other times, he had suffered similar bouts accompanied by horrible headaches, but never this violently.

From that moment on, Bernardo did not lift his head. To improve his health, we took him to the neighboring town of San Angel, which was on a hillside and where it was cooler than in the city. But, since he was still unwell, we returned to the palace, where at least we could count on a group of physicians, although none of them managed to diagnose his illness. Neither could they administer an adequate remedy to make him feel better. When one of them proposed placing some leeches on him, I absolutely refused because I knew those bloodsuckers horrified him. Besides, he had already become too weak from the vomiting and diarrhea to suffer more loss of blood.

Since the patient was not improving as expected, all the court judges, friars from the various religious orders and members of the Inquisition gathered at the palace. On seeing them there all dressed in mourning in the patient's waiting room, I had the sensation that they had not come to bring him the Sacraments but to celebrate his funeral. I felt a chill on seeing members of the Acordada Court, who I had seen on several occasions marching in processions accompanying condemned prisoners to the gallows; they were the same ones who had howled when my husband pardoned those doomed men.

When I was allowed to go into his room, I saw that against the doctors' orders, Bernardo had left his bed and had put on his captain general uniform, his sword and his medals, and was preparing to take the Sacrament of Extreme Unction while standing as a military commander should. I could not help but remember another occasion when Bernardo had received Extreme Unction and that after having married him *in articulo mortis,* we had made love until dawn. Unfortunately, on this occasion the miracle of resurrection would not be repeated.

Nevertheless, the next morning the doctors observed a slight improvement, which I took advantage of to take him on a trip to Tacubaya, because I knew Bernardo did not like the residence at the central plaza. I was happy thinking we would soon be moving to Chapultepec Castle. We decided to stay at the archbishop's palace in Tacubaya, where the archbishop offered to take his confession and administer Extreme Unction. Bernardo, who had not lost his sense of humor, not even as he was dying, told the prelate he wanted me to listen to his confession first. I noted that he was so weak that he had to make a real effort to speak, but thanks to his strong will and his indomitable pride, he spoke to me in a perfectly clear voice.

"Dearest Felicitas, when I told the archbishop that I needed to make my confession to you first, I was not joking. For some time now, I've wanted to speak to you about a certain matter, but on the one hand, I was hard-pressed to tell you something that would upset you, and later this damned illness got in the way. But before I get into that, I have to tell you something odd about my illness. You know that the doctors have not managed to diagnose the illness. I think it could be the result of a wound that healed wrong, like the one I received in my gut during the siege of Pensacola. The surgeon who attended me then told me that if the bullet were not extracted immediately, it could keep burrowing into my abdomen, but under the conditions in the camp, he did not dare operate."

Bernardo straightened up a bit in his chair and looked me directly in the eyes before saying, "I assume that one of the witches you consult in the Parian market stalls has probably told you someone has decided to assassinate me and that I'm being poisoned."

I did not dare confirm that one of the Indian women selling fruit had warned me someone was planning to kill my husband. I had thought that was just to scare me so that I'd give her charity. What began to worry me more was noting that other healers whom I trusted more than her seemed to be avoiding me, as if they knew something. Perhaps it was to protect me from bad news, because they knew I was nearing my due date.

"Well," continued Bernardo, "in any case, you've done very well not falling for that gossip. In case you don't know, I'll tell you there are those who believe that I would use the warmth the people have shown us—and I say, 'us' because you too have become much beloved in this place—to grab power and break Mexico's ties with Spain."

My face probably showed such astonishment that Bernardo grabbed my hand to calm me down. "Don't worry, because as much as I don't agree with the policy that Madrid has adopted towards the viceroyalty, and as much as I sometimes rail and hurl abuse at some ministers and sometimes at the King himself, I would never bite the hand that has been feeding me since I was a child. Another thing is that some people may have used the incident with the government, after I pardoned the prisoners condemned to death, to proclaim to the four winds that I've fallen out of my uncle's good graces."

I had heard this before and I could not help but ask him, "And it's not true?"

"It's a half truth, which is what gossips use to promote all sorts of tall tales."

Bernardo paused to sip some water and catch his breath, as he was tired from speaking. "Felicitas, I well know you are a quick witted and intelligent woman. Needless to say, the relationship between my uncle and me has been rocky at times. In principle, I should be profoundly grateful for the way he's supported me in difficult times and has promoted my military career. But sometimes it pains me that he throws a shadow over all I do, so that whatever I achieve is always chalked up to Don José's influence and benevolence."

"Well, if you'll let me, I'm going to make another observation, which perhaps you yourself have felt or maybe not. Sometimes, by the way he looks at you and how he reacts when you speak to him, I have the sensation that your Uncle José, although he appreciates you and even admires you, he does feel a bit of envy or jealousy, perhaps due to your kindness and your charisma, virtues which he lacks."

"Let's not fool ourselves. If Uncle José had decided that my position here were prejudicial to the viceroyalty's good order and prosperity, he wouldn't hesitate even a second in removing me and, if necessary, having me arrested. I am aware my uncle is capable of committing ignoble acts when he believes he's doing so in the service of the King and indirectly to God. But I know Uncle José has never lost confidence in me. I've even been told that his official ratification of the pardon that I perhaps granted imprudently will arrive in the next dispatch."

"I'm glad you have renewed your relationship with your uncle because, despite his flaws, I think we owe him a lot."

"Yes, but what I wanted to confess to you bears no relationship to my uncle or to the rumors that I'm being poisoned."

"How dare they make an attempt on your life!"

"Those who are involved in this conspiracy are the same ones who came to the palace to see me take Communion a few days ago: members of the Inquisition, the Acordada judges and that whole band of good-for-nothings who are only worried about defending their privileges. But what that gang of imbeciles doesn't realize is that if I could send a spy to the English fort in Pensacola, I would easily discover a plot being hatched under my very nose. But that isn't what I wanted to talk to you about."

Noting that Bernardo was exhausted by his effort to speak to me, I asked him please to rest a few minutes. I arranged two pillows in his easy chair so he could sit up at a better angle. When he leaned too far back, the phlegm filled his lungs and made it difficult for him to breathe. When he reclined his head on the cushions, he half-closed his eyes and, for a few minutes that seemed to last forever, he remained still, resting.

CHAPTER 57

The Quicksilver Statue

(Felicitas St. Maxent continues)

I feared Bernardo would not wake again, but after a while he opened his eyes. From that moment on, his voice sounded stronger and clearer.

"My dear Felicitas, for a time now I've wanted to tell you something, but I've never found the time to do it. Do you remember that a few months ago I traveled to Guanajuato to see how the silver mines were performing?"

"Yes, I remember. . . . You returned so tired and in such a foul mood, you wouldn't tell me anything about your trip. I felt you were hiding something."

"I see you are still a bit of a witch, because it's true: I did have something to hide. You'll recall that soon after beginning our courtship you spoke to me about a witch's vision. She warned you I had committed a sin in the past and that I should redeem myself to avoid having the Father of Waters become angry with me."

I nodded in agreement. I didn't want to interrupt him for fear Bernardo would lose track of what he was saying.

"At that moment, I thought it was a crazy idea. But as time passed, I realized what the witch had told you was true. I had committed a sin, though unconsciously. Here my somewhat problematic relationship with Uncle José rears its head: he abused our family ties by ordering me to the Almadén mines to speak to one of the prisoners, a former memorialist of my acquaintance. He wanted me to obtain from him a document in his possession that could have put my uncle in a com-

238

promising position. I shouldn't have accepted the mission, but the fact is I did, and I succeeded in getting the memorialist to give me the troublesome document voluntarily. What I didn't understand was that in handing over that piece of paper, the man was losing the only guarantee that he would not be harmed. No one dared kill him before retrieving the document from him."

Bernardo paused and asked me to bring a glass of water to his lips. Then he continued. "I should have made sure that, once he gave me the document, my uncle's henchmen would not harm him. But, due to a series of circumstances, I didn't follow through. On returning to Madrid, I asked Uncle José what would become of the man. My uncle responded evasively. and I didn't have the courage to insist."

Bernardo remained silent for a few minutes. I understood he was making a superhuman effort to express himself. "Actually, the more I think about it, the more I realize my appointment as governor was how my uncle had repaid me for carrying out the mission in Almadén. It turned out to have been a shameful assignment."

Bernardo was overcome by a coughing attack. I would have gladly asked him not to speak, because he had already told me a lot, but it was evident that he wanted to get to the end of his story.

"Although it seems impossible, until just a couple of weeks ago when I traveled to Guanajuato, I didn't know for certain what the memorialist's fate had been. In one of my visits to the mine, I thought I recognized the face of one of the foremen managing the operation, and I noticed he recognized me too. It turned out he was the warden of the Almadén Prison, precisely the person to whom my uncle had entrusted the memorialist's custody."

Bernardo's voice had become almost inaudible, but I got closer to him as if I were really listening to his confession.

"It was very difficult to persuade the former warden to tell me what had happened to the memorialist, but he ended up telling me that there had been a terrible fire in the mine, possibly set by the prisoners themselves. Several of them died from asphyxiation, unable to escape from the mine's tunnels. After putting out the fire, the guards took a headcount of the prisoners and realized that the elderly memorialist, much too ill and too old to attempt an escape, was missing. After searching for a time, they found his body at the bottom of a quicksilver deposit, where apparently his murderers had thrown his cadaver to hide their crime. It appeared that when they tried to remove his body, the ore had penetrated his body in such a way that he was completely stiff, turned into a quicksilver statue."

Bernardo closed his eyes and I noticed that tears were running down his emaciated cheeks. But I also saw the relief he felt in telling me this story after so many years.

I should have respected his silence, but couldn't help but exclaim, "Bernardo, you should not feel guilty about his death. You were not the one who ordered the memorialist killed. From what you've told me, you weren't even sure he was going to be killed, although you might have suspected as much."

"I feel guilty of the sin of omission. I should have made sure that once he gave me the manuscript, his life would be safeguarded. The fact is that for many years I've been wracked with uncertainty and anguish about what happened. I did not know for sure until a few weeks ago during my trip to Guanajuato. If ever you return to New Orleans, you can tell your witch that I've already paid for that sin, so the Father of Waters can leave me in peace."

Bernardo raised his hand to point to the rain that had begun to fall forcefully on the windows of the archbishop's palace. But he could not complete the gesture. When I went to close his eyelids with my hand, I realized they had become completely stiff, like the quicksilver statue he had just mentioned.

Epilogue

Four years after the death of Bernardo de Gálvez, Gardoqui still had not made any headway in the mission that Floridablanca had entrusted to him concerning the exclusive use of the Mississippi and the question of Louisiana's northern borders. Therefore, he requested Madrid's authorization to return to Spain.

During the time Gardoqui had spent as a negotiator in the United States, he had maintained a good relationship with Secretary of State John Jay—possibly currying favor with gifts for him or for his wife—and had even developed friendly relations with George Washington himself. The Spanish diplomat was never able to get a commitment from the US Congress, owing, above all, to the southern states' complete opposition. They not only refused to recognize Spanish territorial borders but also offered thinly veiled encouragement to colonists and adventurers to encroach on the border zone.

As a farewell gift to John Jay, Gardoqui had an Andalusian stallion brought to the United States on the Spanish Royal brigantine, the Galvezton. He tarried before leaving so he could be present at the reception Congress was preparing in New York for George Washington, who had been elected the first president of the United States. Gardoqui took advantage of the Galvezton's presence in New York harbor and had it participate in the grand naval parade organized in honor of the new president. Later, he would describe this important event: "(His Excellency George Washington) was received in Elizabethtown by a group of senators and five Congressional representatives, with whom he embarked on a fanciful barge built especially so His Excellency could cross the bay. . . . After his Excellency had arrived about half way to the warship H.C.M. Galvezton, anchored at the junction of the northern and eastern rivers, the ship saluted Washington with fifteen cannon blasts, five cheers of 'Long Live the King of Spain' and other accolades . . . " as the barge passed by.

More than eight years had passed since the siege of the English fort at Pensacola, but hardly anyone remembered Bernardo de Gálvez's feat of sailing his brigantine unharmed under the very nose of the Red Cliffs batteries.

However, if at that time the officer and gentleman from Málaga had not dared crash the port of one of the most important English bastions on the Gulf of Mexico, it's likely the American conflict would have taken a different path and George Washington would not have then been taking the oath of office as the first president of the United States.

Timeline

Bernardo de Gálvez and His Era

This is a broad chronology to help the reader contextualize Bernardo de Gálvez, his home life, and the events that influenced his life.

1716. Marriage of Antonio de Gálvez y Carvajal and Doña Ana Gallardo y Cabrera (Bernardo de Gálvez's grandparents).

1720. Birth of José Bernardo de Gálvez y Gallardo (brother to first-born Matías, Bernardo's father).

1741. After receiving a scholarship to study at the St. Sebastian School in Málaga, José de Gálvez y Gallardo leaves for the University of Salamanca to study law.

1745. Marriage of Matías de Gálvez y Gallardo and his cousin Doña María Josefa de Madrid Gallardo.

1746. Birth of Bernardo Vicente Apolinar, first-born son of the couple.

1755. The French and Indian War begins. In this conflict, England and France initially struggle for supremacy in Europe and America.

1759. Charles III is received in Madrid as King of Spain and the Indies.

1761. Under the terms of the Third Familial Pact, Spain is dragged into a war between France and England, which in large part is unleashed in their respective colonies in North America.

1762. After declaring war on Spain, England captures Havana and Manila.

1763. The Treaty of Paris ends the French and Indian War. Spain recovers Havana and Manila but must cede Florida to England. To compensate for this loss, France cedes the Louisiana Territory to Spain. In Madrid, the Count of Aranda presides over the Military Court Marshal of those responsible for the loss of Havana.

1764. After profound disagreements between the English Parliament and the representatives of the British colonies in North America, London passes laws, which their colonial subjects brand as "Intolerable Acts."

1765. After his appointment as Inspector General of the Viceroyalty of New Spain, José de Gálvez Gallardo sails for Mexico.

1766. The Esquilache Rebellion triggers the dismissal of Charles III's Prime Minister, and the Count of Aranda assumes the presidency of the Council of Castile.

1767. By Royal Decree in Madrid, the Jesuits are banished in April. A few months later, the Royal Decree arrives in Mexico, and Inspector General José de Gálvez carries out the order, harshly putting down popular discontent arising from the expulsion.

1769. Bernardo de Gálvez is ordered to Nueva Vizcaya (New Biscay, Mexico). Inspector General José de Gálvez y Gallardo travels to Sonora, where he fails in his attempts to pacify the Seris Indians of Cerro Prieto. As a result of the campaign's harshness and not having achieved his objectives, Inspector General José de Gálvez suffers a mysterious malady that some witnesses, including memorialist Juan Manuel Viniegra, who oversaw keeps the expedition's diary, describe as an attack of madness.

1770. In Chihuahua, Bernardo de Gálvez is ordered to fight the Apaches, carrying out several campaigns that take him to Texas and New Mexico. When he is alerted to José de Gálvez y Gallardo's precarious health, he rushes to Sonora and accompanies his uncle on his return trip to Mexico and later returns to Spain with the Inspector General after completing his mission.

1772. Once he has returned to Spain, Bernardo de Gálvez is ordered to join the Cantabrian regiment in Pau (France). During his three years there, he perfects his knowledge of military tactics and becomes fluent in French.

1773. In the port of Boston (Massachusetts), a group of white colonists (the Sons of Liberty) disguised as Indians throw newly arrived chests of tea overboard to protest the English Crown's tea monopoly. This action is known as the "Boston Tea Party."

1774. In France, Louis XVI succeeds his grandfather, Louis XV.

1775. In June, the Battle of Bunker Hill is fought between English troops and colonial rebels. This battle is considered the beginning of the War of Independence from England of the thirteen colonies. In July, Bernardo de Gálvez participates in the disastrous campaign against Algiers, where he is seriously wounded, but is promoted Lieutenant Colonel. Afterwards, he is sent to the Avila Military School.

1776. In January, Charles III names José de Gálvez y Gallardo Secretary of State for Affairs in the Indies (Minister for the Indies) that includes broad powers over many aspects in the overseas territories. Among other responsibilities, the minister is also the General Superintendent of Quicksilver. Quicksilver is essential for extracting silver and gold in Spanish America. In May, Bernardo de Gálvez is ordered to report as Colonel of the Louisiana Standing Regiment. Later he will be appointed the interim governor of Louisiana. In July, the Declaration of Independence of the United States from Great Britain is signed in Philadelphia.

In November, José de Gálvez y Gallardo marries Doña María de la Concepción de Valenzuela, the Count of Puebla's daughter. This is his third marriage. In December, Benjamín Franklin arrives in Paris; at the end of the month, the delegation consisting of Franklin, Silas Dean and Arthur Lee have an audience with the French Foreign

Minister, the Count of Vergennes, and, at Vergennes' request, with the Spanish Ambassador, the Count of Aranda.

1777. In January, for the second time the Count of Aranda receives Franklin and the other American delegates, who propose a reciprocal trade agreement between Spain and the United States. After taking possession of his office in Louisiana, Bernardo de Gálvez begins to send arms and supplies to the rebel army, confiscates English ships plying contraband on the Mississippi and orders the English residents in Louisiana to abandon the territory. In February, Arthur Lee, one of the American commissioners in Paris, decides to travel to Spain without prior approval from the Madrid government. He is detained in Burgos, where he meets with the outgoing Spanish Secretary of State Jerónimo Grimaldi, and with Diego Gardoqui, a merchant from Bilbao, who acts as interpreter and mediator in their conversations. Lee succeeds in negotiating Spanish aid to the rebel colonies with the retiring secretary of state, but fearing a diplomatic incident with the English Ambassador, the latter does not authorize his visit to Madrid, where he had wanted to speak with the King. In October, the insurgent army defeats British General Burgoyne at the Battle of Saratoga. This victory prompts France to recognize the rebel colonists and justifies the Spanish Ambassador's recommendation in Paris for the Spanish government to sign an accord with the congressional delegates. The new secretary of state, the Count of Floridablanca, rejects Aranda's recommendation. In October, a Spanish-Portuguese treaty is signed at the San Ildefonso Farm that resolves the Sacramento issue and other border issues between Portugal and Spain in South America. This allows Spain greater freedom on the American Continent and smooths the way for Spain's participation in the colonies' war of independence from England. In November, Bernardo de Gálvez marries the widow Felicitas de St. Maxent *in articulo mortis* in New Orleans.

1778. José de Gálvez y Gallardo succeeds in having the Ordinances of Free Trade with America passed, thereby breaking the former monopoly of American commerce with some Spanish cities.

1779. In May, Madrid informs the provincial governors that the king has decided to declare war on Great Britain, a declaration formalized in June. In August, when Bernardo de Gálvez is preparing for a military campaign on the Mississippi River, a terrible storm strikes New Orleans and sinks the very ships that had already been armed for that campaign. In September, Bernardo de Gálvez's troops invaded the left bank of the Mississippi and capture the English forts of Manchac, Baton Rouge, Panmure and Natchez. By December, Spain wins control of the lower Mississippi Basin. Bernardo de Gálvez is promoted to Field Marshal.

Also in September, the American Congress appoints John Jay as the United States' chief negotiator with the Madrid government.

1780. In March, when Bernardo de Gálvez boards his troops in New Orleans for Mobile, another heavy storm makes the ships run aground, but he succeeds in repairing them to attack Fort Charlotte, which allows him to take Mobile. In May, the first expedition to conquer Pensacola fails when a hurricane breaks up the squadron led by Gálvez. In October, a hurricane also strikes the second expedition sailing from Havana to Pensacola.

1781. In February while leaving Havana with the third expedition to Pensacola, Gálvez succeeds in arriving at the mouth of Pensacola Bay with enough ground troops and a fleet of war ships under the command of Captain José Calvo de Irazábal. In March, José Calvo de Irazábal refuses to have the ships under his command attempt to cross this narrow channel. This puts the safety of the troops already landed on the island of Santa Rosa in danger. Gálvez boards the small brigantine Galvezton and succeeds in breeching the port, despite heavy cannon fire from the English batteries at Red Cliffs. Following his example the next day, the ships of the fleet enter the bay. In May, after a long siege, Bernardo de Gálvez takes Pensacola. This means Spain now controls the two Floridas and the Gulf of Mexico, thus achieving the objectives of his war strategy in that region. In turn, this will allow the American rebel army to concentrate on its struggle against England in the North. In October, General Cornwallis surrenders at Yorktown, a battle in which Spanish troops do not participate. However, Royal Commissioner Francisco Saavedra has a million *pesos* delivered to the head of the French fleet.

1782. Bernardo de Gálvez is appointed head of joint French-Spanish operations to attack Jamaica and moves to the island of Guarico in the French part of the island of Santo Domingo.

In April, Admiral De Grasse's French fleet, which departed from Martinique to join other forces in Guarico, is intercepted by Admiral Rodney's fleet. Rodney succeeds in sinking or taking most of the French ships, including Admiral De Grasse's flag ship. This is the death blow for military operations to take Jamaica. In May, the Captain General of Cuba, Juan Manuel de Cajigal takes the Bahama Islands; Colonel Francisco de Miranda, Cajigal's adjutant, intervenes in the surrender of Nassau. Without having been recognized as a diplomatic representative or ever having been received by King Charles III, John Jay leaves Spain for Paris to reinforce the negotiating team headed by Benjamin Franklin. In September, Bernardo de Gálvez's only son, Miguel de Gálvez y St. Maxent, is born on Guarico.

1783. In January, the Count d'Estaing relieves Bernardo de Gálvez as head of joint operations in the Caribbean. The preliminary preparations for the peace treaty between Spain and Great Britain are undertaken. In April, Matías de Gálvez y Gallardo is appointed Viceroy of New Spain. In September, the Peace Treaty of Paris is signed in which Spain recognizes the independence of the United States. However, the parties do not sign any agreement concerning navigation on the Mississippi or concerning the borders of territories taken by the English. After signing this treaty, John Jay is appointed secretary of state of the United States.

1784 In April, after an absence of eight years, Bernardo de Gálvez returns to Spain with the title of Viscount of Galvezton and Count of Gálvez. He incorporates into his coat of arms the emblem of the brigantine Galvezton, with which he had breached the entrance to Pensacola Bay, and the legend "Yo Solo" (I Alone) is inscribed on his coat of arms.

Gálvez is appointed Inspector General of Veteran Troops and Regulated Militias of the Indies. Diego María de Gardoqui is appointed Spanish *charge d'affaires* in Philadelphia with the difficult mission of negotiating the right of navigation on the Mississippi and the establishment of Louisiana's borders with the United States. In October, José de Gálvez y Gallardo receives the title of Viscount of Sinaloa and Marquis of Sonora. In November, Matías de Gálvez y Gallardo dies in Mexico.

In February, Bernardo de Gálvez is appointed captain general of Cuba. He meets with Diego de Gardoqui in Havana to coordinate a plan of action concerning the United States. In May, Bernardo de Gálvez is appointed the Viceroy of New Spain and lands in Veracruz, where he is received warmly all along the route to Mexico City.

1786. In November, after a mysterious illness, Viceroy Bernardo de Gálvez dies in the archbishop's palace in Tacubaya (Mexico City). In his brief term as viceroy, he has become very popular in New Spain for his advanced and progressive policies.

1787. In May, George Washington is elected the first president of the United States. In New York, Diego de Gardoqui, who has been unable to achieve any of his mission's objectives, attends the celebration of Washington's swearing in, before leaving for Spain. In June, José de Gálvez y Gallardo dies in Aranjuez, Spain.

1788. In December, King Charles III dies.

1795. During Charles IV's reign, Spain yields to all the United States' claims by recognizing the 31st Parallel (instead of the 35th that Gálvez advocated) as the northern Louisiana border and granting the right of free navigation on the Mississippi in a treaty with the United States signed by Spanish Prime Minister Manuel Godoy and American diplomat Charles Pinckney at El Escorial (Spain).